Eliza Pitkin is a filmmaker, journalist and first-time writer. Born by the coast of England in Brighton, from an embryo to an 8-year old, Eliza spent playing dress-up and collecting insects from her small concrete garden. One day her family and her packed up their bags and moved to Shropshire, or what she often refers to as 'the middle of nowhere.' A place of pure tranquility, greenery, and space. The contrast of these two worlds is where the nature of playing and storytelling became translated through pen and paper. Inspired by artists, poets, rebels, human nature, and culture, Eliza discovered her language in poetry. Now residing in London, she is driven by her larger purpose in life which is to enhance the way we communicate, inspire more conviction and conscious awareness in the way we live our daily lives.

ELIZA PITKIN

Rhubarb & Revelations

Rhubarb & Revelations is a collection of poems, prose, and streams of consciousness' told through the eyes of a young person with a gritty, honest, dreamy, and raw take on the human experience.

dedicated to my mum, thanks for life

(in more ways than one)

SPURTS
(and their poems)

Each chapter is titled a 'spurt'

Introduction | 15

I just feel like | 18

Poison over Passion | 20
Broken-Hearted People Club | 21
Home Remedy | 22
The Magician | 24
All the best parts | 27
Just the Mourning(s) | 28
Somewhere along the way | 30
Demon in the dark | 31
Finding the self | 32
Smoke in my head | 34
To love me | 35
My Gallery | 36
Bad Habit | 37
Then what? | 38
Dear G | 39
Got sent off in an ambulance the day after my break up and the paramedic asked me on a date, it felt inappropriate | 40
My first period after you | 41

That's a lot to process | 42

Stereotypes are real | 44
Sofa | 48
Put it down | 49
Body Hair | 50
Soul Mate | 52

I only exist | 54
Relation | 55
Female Effect | 56
Labelling and Grouping | 57
That's Me | 58
Lemon Curd | 61
Rain | 62
Crossroads | 63
Chaos and Peace | 64
Dating | 65
I think about it all the time | 66
We'll be buck, probably | 68
My own split personality | 69
No one can see me | 70
Sacred Geometry | 71

Just came online | 72

Teenage Oppression / Obsession | 74
Rooms | 75
Things that hang | 76
REM | 78
Porn | 79
Something lifted from an erotic story I wrote when I was 14 | 80
Life as a Sim | 81
Dream Being | 82
My Biggest Fan | 83
Parasite. | 84
Time | 85
Dear | 86
You're the only one | 87
Self Declaration | 88
Connection | 89
A Fallacy | 90
One way ticket to the multi-verse | 91
Aegosexual | 92
Disgusted | 93
Multiple Lives | 94
Spaces | 95
Plant | 96

Give me some meaning | 98
Lovelife | 99
Losing Grip | 100
You are all of it | 101
Loading | 102
Just to update you | 103

Hope you're well | 104

Future Self | 106
When the milk separates | 107
Middle of a sentence | 108
Disperse | 109
Mermaid | 110
In love with a promise | 111
Time Travelling | 112
Thoughts | 113
Soul Sister | 114
Clutter | 115
That's a bit deep for the dinner table | 116
Let's talk about why | 118
Empathy | 119
Angel | 120
The Gooey Bit | 121
Passing Feeling | 122
Toolbox | 123
"Nature" | 124
Happy u exist | 126
Please like me again | 127

I've been thinking | 128

DM | 130
How to be a good lover | 131
DNA | 132
Stubbed toe | 133
Commit | 134
Dear his mum and dad | 136
21st Century Salesmen | 138
Donut | 139

I'm a dick | 140
The Work | 141
The Weather | 142
Fetish for expression | 143
Trigger | 144
Vacancy | 145
My Choice | 146
To the facilitators | 147
At your fingertips | 148
Enter Thought / Enough company for one | 149
Campers | 150
Here to annoy us | 151
Your Memory | 152
Breaking up with someone who can't help themselves is difficult | 153
Wrinkles | 154
"I hate that word" | 155
I AM U | 156
One of the answers | 157

Warm Wishes | 158

You temp | 160
Wisdom from this experience | 161
It feels personal | 162
Spectrums | 163
Adults | 164
Just Listen | 165
Things that fly | 166
Colour in | 167
'Old' Me | 168
Cookie Jar | 169
DIY | 170
A human complete | 171
Let's make self respect sexy again | 174
How Life happened to you | 175
What If | 176
How it was before | 177
Look Up | 178
Utopia | 179

Reporters | 180
A Bundle | 181
To my other spoon | 182
The Cost | 183
Honey | 184
Addicts | 185
Maleness | 186
The Entanglement | 188
Self Reflect | 189
'Myself' | 190
Ego | 191
What're the chances? | 192
The End of the World | 193
Hands | 196
Vote | 197
Meditation | 198
A Generation | 200
It's gone viral | *201*
I Believe | 206
The great excursion | 207
Born again | 208
I'll wake up | 209
Every interaction you have | 210
Choice | 211
Lift me up | 212
Miracles | 213
Seasons | 214
Evolution | 215

introduction

Welcome to my poetic diary.

Thank you for having this book, assuming you bought it rather than steal, borrow, happen upon, or just skimming through - either way, I appreciate your presence.

I created this book during lockdown. Between overeating, binge-watching, random walks, ruminating over the past, and navigating around my parents' house, I found moments to put together all the poetry I had written over the years.

The lockdown experience inspired the title of the book, Rhubarb and Revelations. I was convinced this apocalyptic and unnerving reality of lockdown was the beginning of the end of the world, so my family and I built a vegetable patch preparing like doomsday preppers. Amongst the abundance of cabbage, kale, spinach, carrots and cauliflower (that consequently got savagely feasted on by caterpillars), we grew luscious rhubarb. Rhubarb is this bitter vegetable that lends itself to the ever-famous rhubarb and custard combo. This veiny, leafy, bright red, sweet, and sour vegetable felt like a good symbol for the bizarre experience of lockdown, and in many ways, life itself. A bitter sweet thing. Also, in the actor world, rhubarb is a term for background chat, when background actors in a film are miming conversation, they can silently repeat "rhubarb" to make their lips look like they're talking. (To try out this stunt it requires silent miming and a mirror.)

For me the lockdown experience felt surreal, it still does. Suddenly I couldn't help but sense that people became even more divided, fearful, resentful, perhaps unbelieving, and seemed to expose a lot of the unstable structures that our culture had previously revolved around. One big thing lockdown revealed was how much people wanted to share their unknowing and unreliable opinions and predictions about the nature of the virus and the future, I count myself as one of them. It showed us how much we rely on knowing, how much we want to cuddle up safely under the blanket of prediction. It forced us to surrender to the experience; to the lack of movement and all the perturbed dystopian sh*t that's going on. In this space, we grew more knowledge about ourselves, our society and how we respond. In this way, it was bitter but sweet.

Now, for the 'revelations' bit. At the beginning of the lockdown, I tried to seek some comfort and wisdom. Despite not being religious, I read and studied sections of the Bible. The book of Revelations is the final book of the New Testament which conveys imagery of disaster and struggle. However, revelations also refers to the epiphanies and ideas like light bulb moments, a moment of a blissful unveiling of thought, a connection, or an awakening of some kind. So in that way, think of the 'revelations' bit as the custard. This duo-act of definitions created the perfect title for what this book was like to create.

Lockdown was a fascinating experience for all of us to better understand our relationship with the outside world and the external pressures put upon us. We stepped off the spinning hamster wheel and were consequently granted the opportunity to connect with our inner ecosystem. It was a time to re-learn and re-prioritise the structures of ourselves, culture, family, vast social disparities, our curated environment, and our purpose. It was a time for serious re-evaluation. I wrote this book with the intention for it to act as a handbook to help you listen to yourself and your role in the big picture.

This small book you're about to embark upon is somewhat of a diary I have been keeping since I was 18 in the form of poetic thought processes regarding spirituality, mankind, the future of the planet, and the experience of life itself. Treat this as part of a ritual, the following is what I suggest for making your own cosy space to enjoy these pages.

- Sit in a part of your house/flat/room/shed/van that you NEVER usually sit. Make it really comfy. I'm talking; pillows, blankets, and a heater (if you need one).

- Light something up. Have a light source near you such as candles, a torch, fairy lights, or a sidelight. This is something to create new shadows and light.

- Grab yourself a yummy, preferably warm, drink.

- Get a notebook and pen nearby in case you have thoughts or want to scribble onto the book.

- Bring something you love. Maybe invite your sibling, a pet to join, or an object you cherish.
- Wear something comfy.

I hope you find something that feels real for you. Perhaps it will help you channel some pain, excitement, tension, or any other emotion that can help you process something you're going through. When I wrote these poems, it never crossed my mind that I would ever publish them, and yet here we are! Publishing this book is the most personal and exposing thing I have probably ever done. I hope it's worth it.

Disclaimer: I have a very particular style of punctuating my work, for example, I do not always use the first capital letter of a poem, and sometimes I don't title the work, I think it's best throw you into it without preamble or context, in latin, it's called in medias res. Just roll with it and enjoy!

I just feel like

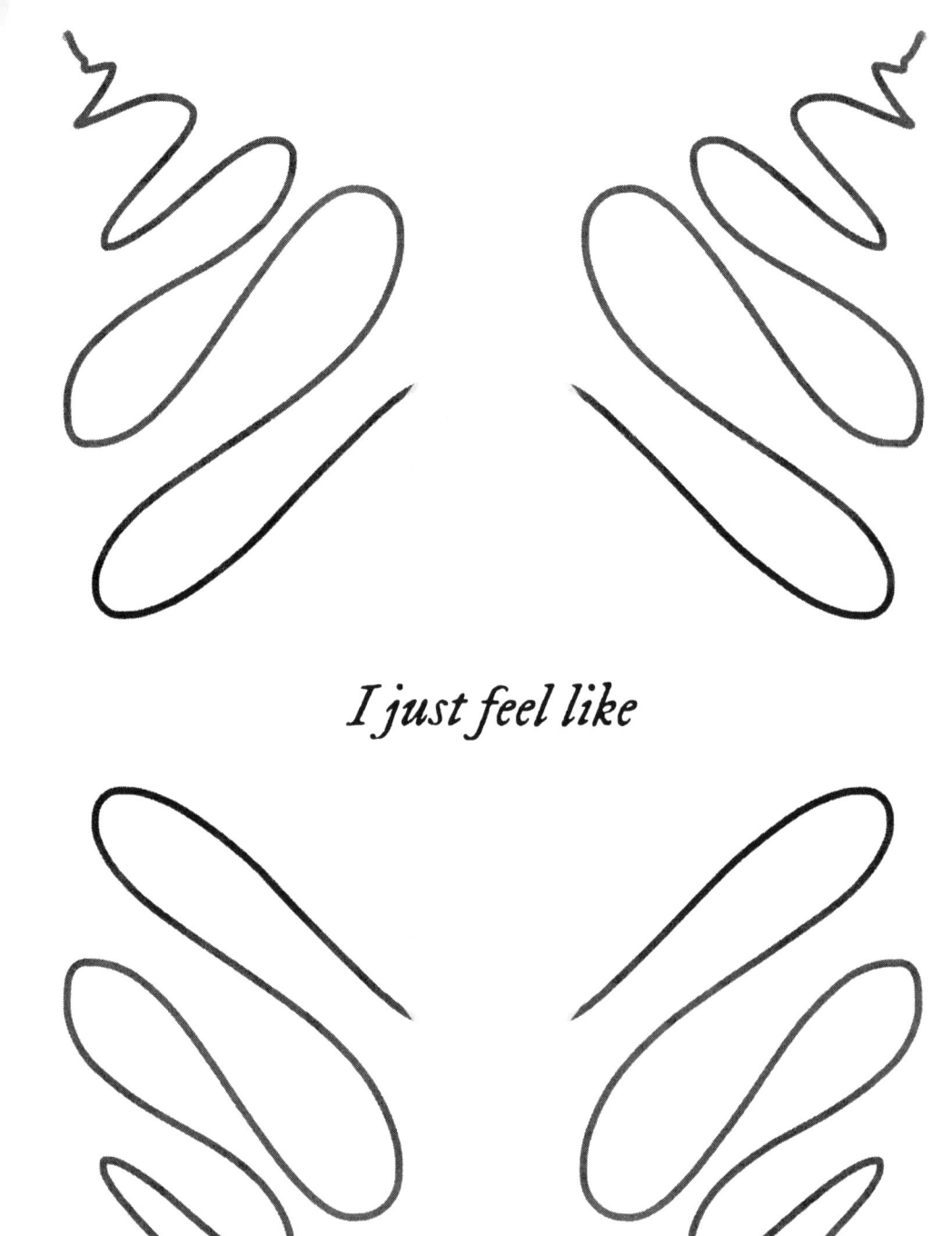

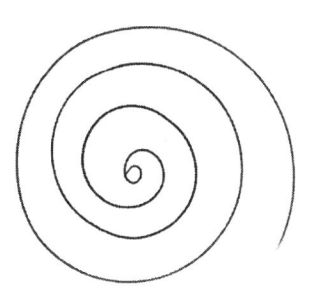

When I was 19 I broke up with my first serious relationship that lasted 3 years, and it was tough. The relationship was as a catalyst to see how myself and my partner were treating eachother, and ultimately ourselves. There were multiple times during that relationship where I didn't act on my instincts which I now understand as me dissolving my 'boundaries'. I had this ingrained compulsion to make the relationship work even at the cost of my own needs. (Which I later discovered was a mirroring of my mother's behaviour…but that's a whole other story). So by the time the relationship did come to an end, I had no clue of who I was, or what I wanted.

My unhappiness caused sleepless nights, disconnection from rooms of people and made me look inward (I know, cliché). The thing was, the more I looked inward, the more I realised that there was no 'me' to look at. I seemed to be looking at nothing. But at the same time, it was everything. I had an outer-body experience which was a turning point, I saw myself from a distance (somehow) and then couldn't help but question, who was the observer and who was "me"?

I came to realise that all I actually seemed to be was nothing more than a sponge that has soaked up a certain life experience, a personality that I'd constructed, and a name and all that. I lost my personality for a long time, and practiced just 'being' instead of 'doing'. In this space, I was emotional, still, observant, and at times, self-destructive. When I visualise this first spurt of the book I imagine damp soil and porous skin.

In this space it sometimes felt like the earth itself was against me. I couldn't feel at home with nature, or the elements, or even feeding myself. I suppose it was depression but I prefer to call it a transformation because it ultimately brought on revelations, ideas, creativity, spirituality and eventually a smooth recovery. In this space, I picked up a pen and wrote the following poems.

she waits
to bathe
his skin
in love,
to drown
the voice saying,
'you're not
    enough'

but **he never** comes
because despite her suffering;
her cries
and sighs

 he still choses the poison
over
the passion
    between   **her**   thighs

I looked around me and saw
all the broken-hearted people.

Compared, compromised, abused and used.

And then I understood,
I had just become a member.

-the broken hearted people club-

- Home Remedy -

After I left.

The hands around pulled me in,
Sprinkled me with salt and sugar
and bathed my skin in vinegar.
Wrapped me in a quilt of silk
and strapped a cloth around my eyes,
and there, I slept.
They delivered a platter of seeds,
 with a spoonful of cream
and begged me to cry.
Grated ginger in my tea
and there, I wept.
I lived in darkness for days,
tightened my skeleton to an embryo,
and painted my purple face pale.
And there, I saw a ghost.

Watched him crawl into the lining of my sheets
and burn his flesh into mine.
 His fingernails scratch my spine,
dig into the bones of my skull
and his tongue taste my food.
And there, he stood on my chest and danced on my belly,
pulled my toes from my torso and cursed my name.

 I spoke in riddles that day,
paced in circles,
Chanted spells.
Howled 'till I was deaf
and drew shapes of hoodoo.
I hung garlic from every window
 Lighting wax in every corner,
and whipped my hands for clemency and there,
I dreamt of many worlds.

Worlds where you still loved me,
And I'd wake with my toes uncurled.
I meditated to my mother's voice
singing lullabies of love.
Listened to her whisper to the spirits and beg for patience,
She turned night to day,
for she too has seen the demon's shadow.
And there, I healed.

The seeds in my stomach grew
Pollen soothed my throat
and flowers bloomed from my mouth.
 The salt healed my wounds
and the sugar sweetened my soul.
 Vinegar peeled my flaking skin
and the cream repaired the poison.
 The tea warmed my blood
and my mother's voice turned
my sorrow to serenity.
And there, under my bed
 I released my demon.
 I opened the blinds.
I read of warriors,
grew coarser skin.
 Smudged red into the walls
and sliced my hair with a knife.
I felt the weight on my feet,
and danced to the heartbeat,
looked in the eyes of my protectors
and shouted my name for recognition.
But every so often,
When all is silent
 I'll close my eyes
With no strap across my lids
 or remedy in my tea.
No demon to be seen,
 I'll see you there, my love.

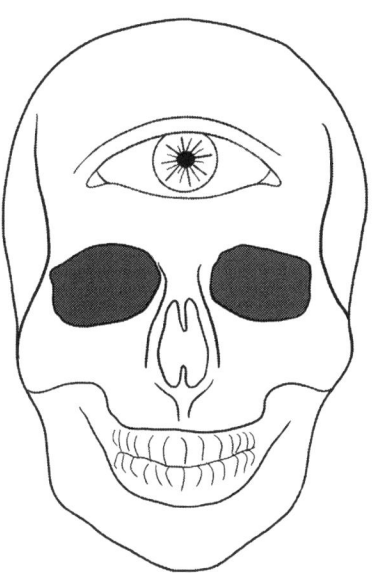

- The Magician -

Did I ever tell you what a great magician he was?
He dries eyes and drops jaws…
Do you know about the wonderful circus show?
It's a hard one to catch, but a place to go!

Drop your ticket money at the door,
and tuck your heavy coat to the floor.

He dances and runs behind wildcats
and pulls rabbits out of hats.
With shiny shoes and a colourful bowtie,
Even the fairest woman is drawn to the glint of his eye
but keep a watch 'cause with a just whisper in the ear,
After a dance and a smile, they'll disappear.

This one's for the weary eyed and abstract,
In stripy clothes and a pointy nose… It's the interval act.
He'll juggle three oranges until you stare,
with just one foot on a ball
and a mandarin in the air.

There is of course, the act for the empathic,
A miming act so needed, so classic.
Ever mimed you're in a box before?
A box of such see-through glass, it's not even there.
A box he can't escape,
Not even you could make a gape.
What it must be like to step into his illusion,
Or is it best to merely watch the delusion?

The air is full of amazement and buttery popcorn scent,
as I wait the night patiently behind the hidden tent.
Peering through a rip in the stalls,
waiting for the final stage call.

A girl with two heads,
a knotted rainbow of dreads.
Hanging from the ceiling to lift higher,
as I jump through hoops of blazing fire,
I twist my waist right round,
and click my bones to the sound.
I split my legs and expand my arms,
Read cards of hope and bedazzle with charms.

Watch him alter his act to the audience's glee,
he is everything that he was meant to be.
If you haven't heard of the magician,
perhaps you've heard of 'the man with two faces?'
He would open up the most glamorous cases,
Pull out and wear masks of fine silk and satin.
One, a mask of distraught eyes and a wide smiling mouth.
All masks hand-painted, some chipped, some cracked,
watch this one, he only appears in the second act!

Or how about, 'the fury?'
With truck wheels twice my size,
a man with only red in his eyes.
A look so fierce,
only his wicked tongue could bring you to tears.
Awake at night,
roaring for a fight.
The audience look away in fear when he stared,
The sight of the scared, for he even frightens his biggest fan,
For that ladies and gents is the 'Fury man!'

And when the show comes to an end,
He packs his case, with another show to attend.
He washes his painted face with a rag,
packing every costume in a bag.
And within moments of the applause, he leaves,
travels the road with the lost, the foreign and the thieves.

The last ball bounces out onto the circus floor,
I couldn't understand how a place could become such a bore.
The seats are left with thorny twigs of what was once petalled,
All laying and watching the sand from the stage left unsettled.
The popcorn smell had changed to the stale stench of liquor,
When he left, the light made a sudden flicker
bouncing off the fallen glitter
From his show, it's all left to sweep,
Where wildcats now all lay to sleep.
The dancers sat in what looked like ashes,
The women rubbed their feet and peeled off their lashes.

                    Who does he become when it's all done?
                  When it's just him in a room, is it all still fun?

Many years later I saw him performing in a street,
Still juggling, miming and hiding things in a sheet.
Some ate their lunch and stared, others stroll past,
distracting their kids from walking too fast.
His face was full of grey and flaking paint,
all the charming props he used to entertain
were now just poor jokes and watery eyes,
and the smiles became excuses for lies and false wealth.
The true sadness was seeing him know himself
as the crowd mirrored his own self neglect.

      'You beautiful actor dressed as a smudged reject,'

I said to myself as I slinked away,
there was nothing left for me to say.
His eyes did not dart to his past support act,
as he focussed on keeping his new show intact.

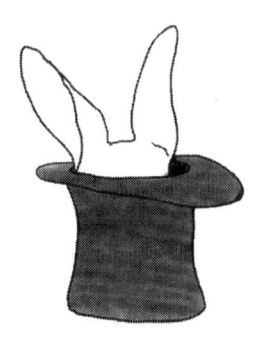

You're all the best parts of me and so much more.

- Just the mourning(s) -

The first morning was strange.
The bed was cold.
I never remember it being *this* cold.
I put extra layers on,
I slept
in socks.

Thinking of what I was so used to;
the line of my spine pressed into the line
of *your stomach,*
My legs on yours.
Our toes entangled,
And the fat off my bottom curled into *you.*
My hair so safely on *your shoulders.*
The tight clasp of your hand on my hip
and *your soft exhales* on my neck.

The next mornings were bizarre.
Where were you?
Suddenly two legs felt so lonely in these sheets,
What pillow did you sleep on?
Do you think of me before the sun rises?

The mornings after that were hard.
I now miss you.
There's only so many pillows I can plump,
dials I can turn for heat,
and weeks
before I have to wash your smell.

The few moments
before I pull myself up were harder,
I would stroke the insides of my thighs
cover my eyes and think of you,
then look outside
and acknowledge this would be
another day;
of realisation
consciousness,
and wanting to hold your jaw and whisper,
Good morning
my love.

Breathe.

I began to sleep on your side,
threw out your toothbrush
and stopped making fresh coffee.

And they were just the mornings,
you *should've* seen me during the nights.

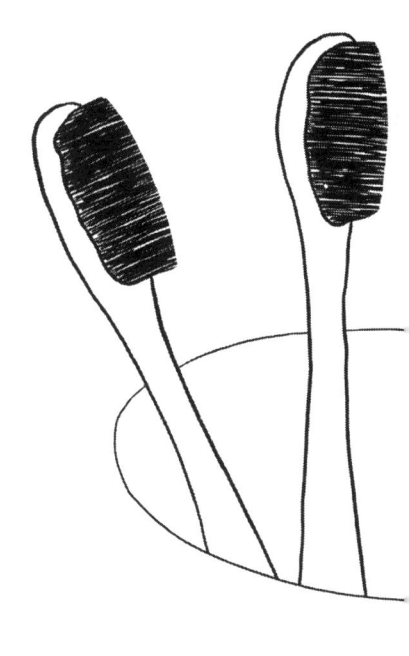

I wasn't heartbroken
because I lost you.

I was heartbroken
because
somewhere along
the way
I lost me.

- Demon in the dark -

You see,
I had fought for you,
Clenched my fists
sucked my teeth
and battled with
doubt.

Like a demon in the dark,

lights were never on long enough
for me to see that you didn't quite exist.

I had stabbed my gut with a sword
and lost my instinct,

you see,
they only existed through the lies they told
and the empty nods of others.

Watch out for people
who live in the dark,
fear loneliness
and prey on the naive,

For when your wisdom comes,
It is you that is left
lonely and
in the dark.

- Finding The Self -

To find me again

I looked for me
Between the sheets of randomers,
Around the salt rim of a glass
and the pop of a bong.

I looked for me
in the depths of the unconscious,
Begging not awake.
I tried to find a purpose
as I stared at the ceiling,

I looked for me
I tried to put a finger on where I was
but felt nothing.

I even looked out of my window
and scrolled through your Facebook
I put a glass to my face,
and tried to find colour in my eyes
I looked through old photos
and tried to recognise my smile.

Every day I looked for myself,
Not for you,
But for me.

You ran off with all the best parts of me,
but they were also pretty, sweet, weak parts of me,
Open and vulnerable like a bleeding wound.

I have thicker skin now,
You'd hate it
It's coarse, rough, strong skin.

And I find myself in
The lines on my hands
The hair on my legs
The comfort of my friends
and the life that is mine.

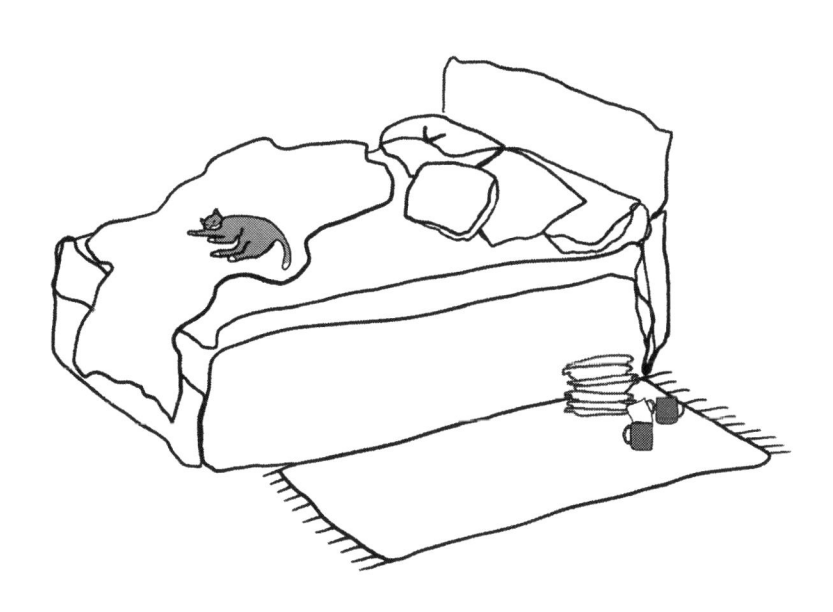

It was as if all that smoke in my head made me see clearly.

I JUST FEEL LIKE

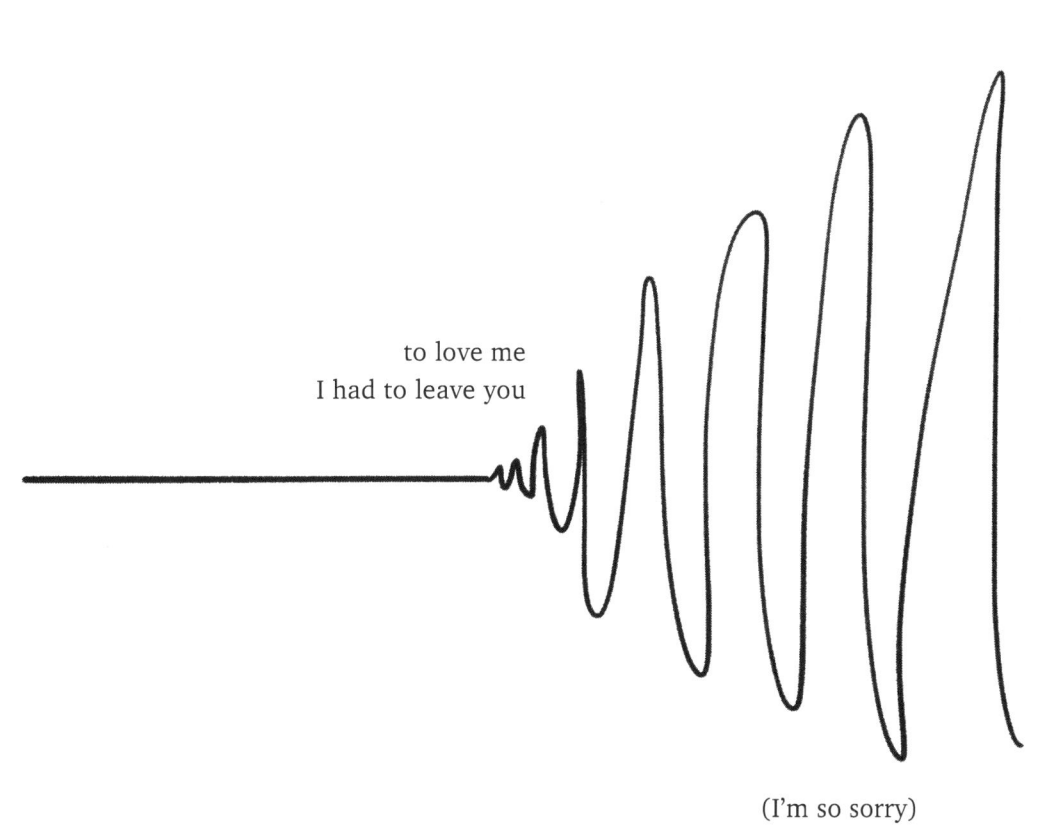

to love me
I had to leave you

(I'm so sorry)

ELIZA PITKIN

- My Gallery -

The day my heart shattered
I hung up broken parts like art
with strands of my fallen hair
Each door a moving mirror,
I potted plants as pathways
and wrote words and words
  of us,
for you.

Then you came back,
I laid you down,
Your boots on the silk.
Read the poems of love
and you drifted off.
I showed my house like a gallery
and you weren't even looking.
I asked you what you felt
and you
said nothing.

Then you kissed me like
any other lad.

You looked out of place
in my house,
next to me,
between my lips,

I see
now,
I'd built a house
from heartbreak
now
too beautiful
for you.

He danced for me with his tongue
strummed me with his fingers
begging for me to make music

He imprinted on me the same act
he had performed on the first lover who faked it.

- A Bad Habit -

What happens to our "*forever*"
when we heal the scars
that put us together?

- Dear G -

I crave to be more mindful;
To expand moments of you into eternity
let them spread lilac across the sky

we are water
moving
washing
crashing
into one another
as soft to touch
and as tough as the ocean
we are cups of tears
and streams of debris.
You live in me.
The single word *of your name* ignites
the flutter in my stomach
and the crack inside my chest
(with all the pieces that you mended).
In a parallel paradise
there is no choice
and time is of
no essence,
no past encounters,
or future floods,
and there
pour into me
my love.
My love for you stuck strong
and yours held for so long,
Hold on, be happy and whole,
let all your true wisdom unfold.

I wish, I regret, I crave
for you
my love,
deeply and always.

My breathing pipes burst
and I felt my heart crack
inside my chest
the morning
after I left.

- November 14th 2017 - (the day I went to the hospital) -

it was a loss in itself
no longer a mutual relief
or a 'what if'
my womb unbridled by your hands
when I cried.
It was official.
Another memory of you
soaked up and flushed away

- my first period after you left -

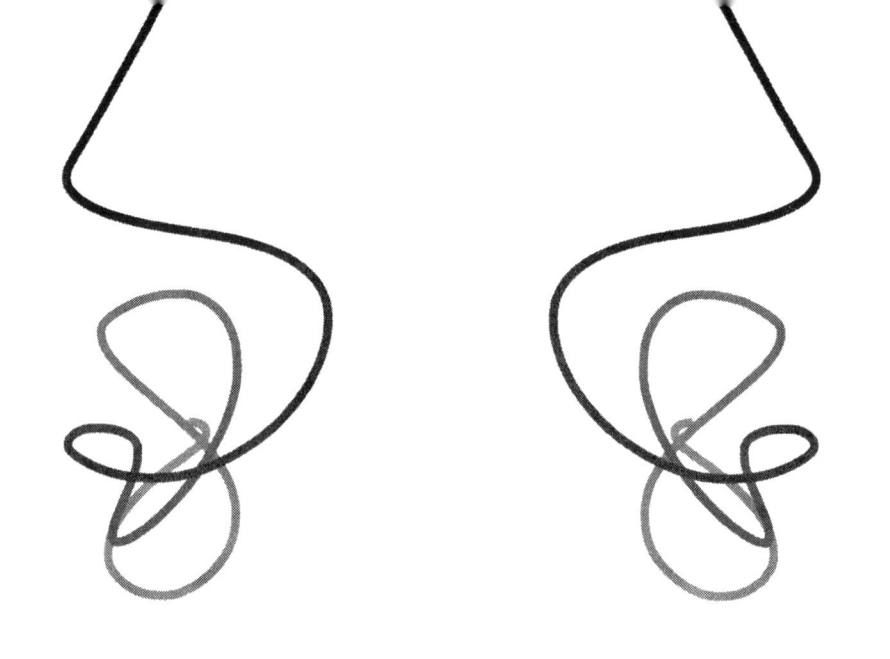

that's a lot to process

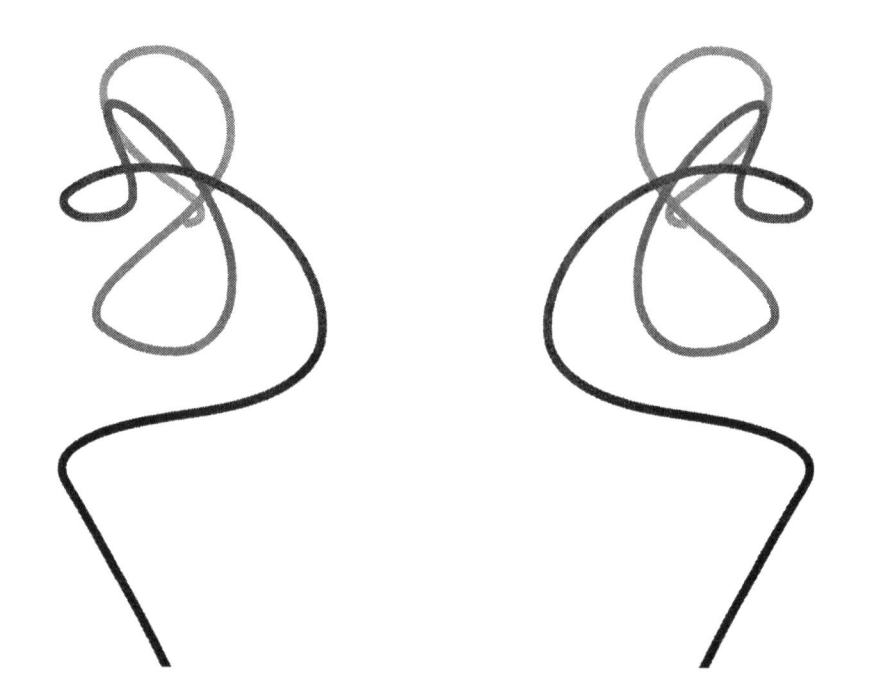

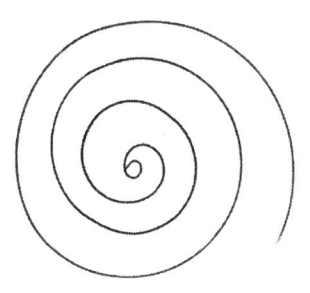

This next spurt is around the time I moved from the countryside to the centre of busy London. I changed my name from Beth to Eliza, this granted me the opportunity to not only change my surroundings but change the literal sound of how I identified.

I kept asking the big unanswerable questions, *What is the point? Why do we exist? What am I? Why am I here? Why is any of this happening?* When you ask yourself these questions enough times, you'll find yourself in a bit of a hole. You also begin to realise how many people don't think about it, which in my case, made me a little paranoid. But I soon realised everyone's trying to find their own purpose, and meaning in some way. These ways include religion, money, self-perfection, fame, politics, exercise, relationships, creativity, recognition, hobbies, trivial pursuits, and so on. During this time I viewed myself more objectively and as a consequence, I began to view others that way too. I was part-time studying with no real friends around me and the only interaction I had was with strangers, colleagues, or customers at my 30-hour-a-week hospitality job. Ultimately this year could've been titled "hello adulthood!" When I read through this next spurt of poems I am aware of a deep sense of loneliness accompanied by a busy mind, in a busy place.

Right now as I write this paragraph I can't help but visualise a shiny blue colour and the texture of concrete.

so here's the deal
- stereotypes are real -
I know because I am one;
a disgusting one.
   I'm white
a bit left,
   a bit right
being green
   eating clean,
A pathological diffuser
A winner and a loser.
raw till 4
   Grass before beer
I'm in the clear,
   I'm fucking
then chucking,
   planting the seeds and
pulling the weeds.
Positive affirmations reinforced
Parents confirmation of divorce
Sort of for it, but I see why not
   downward dog
Head down, ass up,
ruff ruff
smoking pot
puff puff
Avoiding a shot,
Who's about for an
Emotional Fallout?
   Come play the x box,
Before I do my ex
   (in socks)
And sign 'X'
(but out the box

THAT'S A LOT TO PROCESS

I should mention sleep, it's my better life.
Being unconscious has its perks.
Drift off with a movie,
that's how the lucid dream works.

Surrounded by people who care way too much
and I've recently become partial to a coffee rush.
Avoiding the daily grind, my commitment is frothy.
Now I wake up looking like shit,
Nothin' about me is glossy,
Another thing to depend on
Another thing to ween off
all I need now is a themed
mug and a bag
that says, 'coffee is life.'
But I'm not that type.
More like a
Pug and a fag
and a husband called Nial.
Nah, it's all not my style,
It's all pure jokes,
and into child's pose.
Also, I'm in a music video
every time I travel,
Emotions through notes,
another life flows.

A sociopath from my work just quit
And I think my childhood crush is still fit,
Would probably still get it.
It's all nostalgia, I just need a hit
he's a wannabe rapper now,
with Grammarly everyone can be a great writer
That chapter of life now punctuated.
It's probably my hormones.

They've fluctuated.
De Ja Vu
   coffee's shit
don't panic,
'Cause,
    it's organic.

My financial phobia
has become
consumer nervousness
A kinda claustrophobia of
capitalism encircling us.
Don't want it to be purposeless.
'Cause I have issue with good-bye's.
So I'm a "christian…iddist…ual Jedi"
I mostly live for the moments of slumber,
Wishing that I was more than a number.
Whilst I cleanse with rose-water toners,
Affiliating with randomer-loners.
Taking cold showers,
  for more self-belief powers
Mind over matter
  Trying to clear my mind
of all of its tatter
Like a bit of this,
a bit of that.
   Avoiding diet fads
Because don't wanna get fat
So I watch my weight
like the food on my plate
and what comes out my - -
Rimmel
   get the London look

he's all grown up now
inked himself like a Bristol wall
I'm all grown up too
like Alice in wonderland
except porn is the rabbit hole
Sold!
got2be hairspray for a screaming hold
I'm a mumbling worrier
Keeping my head above,
Humble warrior
Learning to self-love
So I can contribute
with no ego.

I think they call that
a *cum tribute.*

"Stay, I'll take the sofa,"
he insisted so chivalrously.
This was an hour before he climbed back into his bed.
Perhaps I didn't look serious enough when I repeated *'no.'*
Here, I watch myself value this stranger's feelings over my own.
Oh, chivalry is dead.

Can you regret something moments before it's happened?

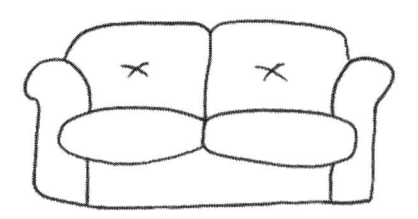

- Put it Down -

I'm a fiddler,
a hair splitting, ring-turning, spot-picking
nail - nibbler.

Look at me, thighs are getting heavy, belly getting round,
Always snacking on something, I can't put it down.
Shovelling information into my mouth like it has no bounds
searching through fridges like the lost and found.

- Body Hair -

It started with me tearing out my hair
and then chopping it with a knife,
I then decided to go full native,
so controversial for my time.

*'She's making a point, she's off the rails
with sparkly paint chipping from her nails,
That upper lip could do with some attention
and thighs are getting heavy, do I dare mention?
Moisturise or you'll go dry
you'll forget to try at such a young age,
your skin will flake and fray,
be more fake for goodness sake.'*

I counted the time it took
to shave my pits
and the money spent
on pink razors and removal kits.
Decided to spend it elsewhere
and gained a repulsion for being bare,
maybe spend more on dental care.
Fuck spending cash on a painful wax.
I'll plug myself with a cup to avoid
the luxury tax.

I claim the hair to save me from friction
At the cost of constant human confliction
Like hetero girls rubbing their porous whiskered legs
As they tell me they prefer it that way,
Because *"it's softer in bed"*
"It's not for the boys"
So I guess it's a choice.
But every time you say you prefer yourself smooth,
You're saying you prefer yourself not being you.
Perhaps it's a choice,

But perhaps it's inbuilt belief that we adopted
and claimed as our own
in the same way we faked our moans, made ourselves
clones and starved ourselves to be skin and bone.
An indoctrination from the sight of porn
and peer pressure
of oppressive patriarchal appetite.
But for me,
to love myself fully
as the soft mammal
and womanly vessel
that I am
feels right.

Here you go men,
I hope you like the female version
of '*a real woman*'.
He says he's surprised himself,
he likes me furry
says it made him feel all pervy,
a man who likes me
all natural and curvy.

Then there was the lockdown,
I haven't plucked an eyebrow since
to reconstruct the way I frown,
seems I express anger with a wince.

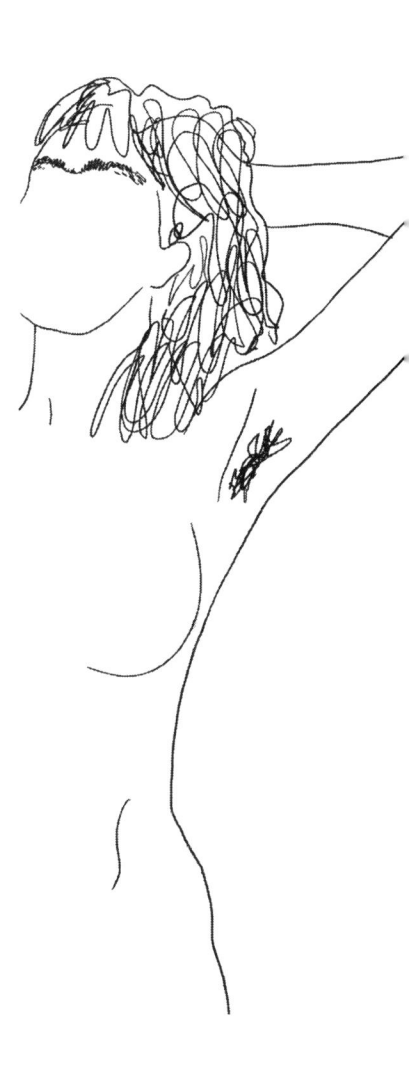

- Soul Mate -

Where the fuck are you?
I moved to a whole other county,
went from bumpkin to towny,
Chopped my hair
(From here to there)
From fringe to a bob
I changed my job
Dumped one friendship group
Made a new friendship group
and just in case you stopped by,
I stopped fucking that one guy.
Left, right on every profile,
another fake, toothy smile,
Swiping through vile lifestyle
From one to the next
Even drafted you a sext.
Going on more dating trials
I've increased my radius miles
All boring ugly faces on every platform.
And do-not-tell me that
this is the '*norm.*'

I find fragments of you scattered
Like puzzle pieces but more tattered;
Saw your coat near Camden,
some long attire with branding.
Your swagger by the Southbank,
cool, convictive, and frank.
A house you'd like in Hackney
tall, sturdy, and wacky.
Your smile somewhere near Kings Cross
but when I looked again, I'm still at a loss.
I searched for you in conversation;
some sense, a laugh or quotation,

So where the fuck are you?

And winter will soon arrive
Another season to survive
Perhaps out there you're lost
Not so easy to find in the frost,
you or the rain?
the rain or you?
The rain and regret,
I lay thinking and fret,
where the fuck you are.
No park, no street nor bar.
I thought you'd be with me for New Year,
meet the family, give 'em the 'all clear'
"see everyone, my better half!"
(The caption on our photograph.)

So I redecorated my room
hung up plants to bloom
Bought a sexy t-shirt you'd like
Saw a statue, it was almost life-like
Masturbation went from a temporary state
to a whole first prize champion gold plate!
Oh had the best pizza, culinary art!
Too much for me so I bagged up your part
ate it two days later when you still weren't here.
Not here,
to endear, to fear
you're nowhere near
I'm here
waiting
anticipating
speed dating
locating
isolating
looking in the flow
Could be now or tomorrow,
Could be any second.

We'd get along I reckon.

I only exist when you're here.

we are wounded and loved in the same way,
a chain of choices made us what we are today.
A child, an observer, a mirror of what we went through
Who would've knew?
Your parents were growing
at the same time as you.

built with pain
quilt with a stain
she wraps her legs 'round
a comfort blanket
a witch hoax
as blood soaks
losing some eggs
Cursing Eve
for her temptation
a bloody week it takes
of tearing sensation
wasted bed sheets
and anxiety when it's late
goosebumps of pain
grief and change
rinse the womb
time for a drain
see what's true
cry and shout
for the drought
makes me proud
makes us connect
this is that female effect

You love labelling people and yourself.
You group them together I've realised,
box 'em up and let it limit you.

I get it, it's easier.
I'd do the same, if I didn't self reflect.

"I don't *feel* it,"
you said.

Now I'm left to *feel* it for the both of us.

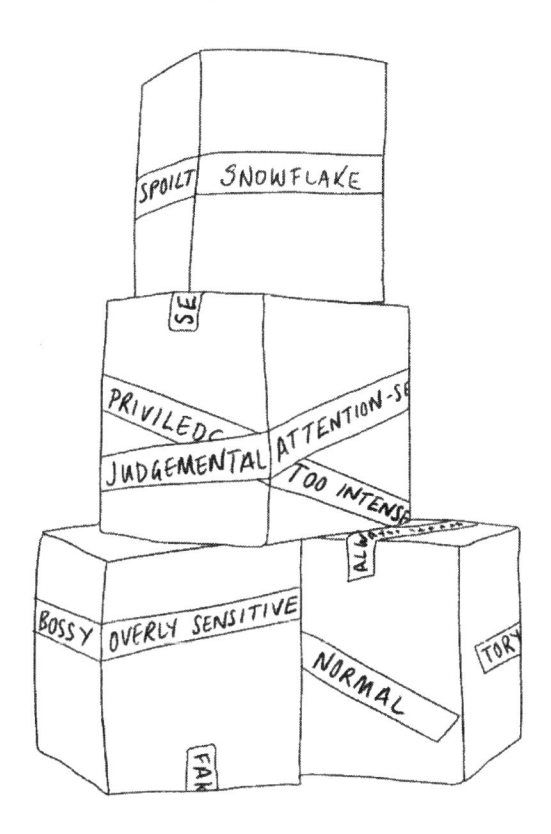

(Sometimes when I'm on the toilet I pretend I'm in a group therapy session and it's my turn to talk because I find comfort in a group but now I realise, I'm still alone on the toilet. This is roughly what I've been saying.)

Hi, I'm Eliza
"Hi Eliza"
I know we're not supposed to use real names,
but fuck it, that's mine,
I have an ironic sense of self,
I guess I'm an escapist,
but it's pretty chronic, which doesn't help.
A kind of introverted extravert;
mind of dirt, bit of an observer
and a little berserk.
Completed with being ascetic
all my own self-set is so strict
'cause I restrict all my pleasures
things like 'no screens past eleven,
food got to be ethical, I know,
it's all a bit radical.
A sort of control-obsessed, self-abusive
addict with allusive disorders
I was trying to throw up food for a while
but the gag reflex was too good for that style.
Saw the spectrum and now I think I'm gay
but maybe I'm just completely colourblind,
keeping myself open for a partner to find.
I think I could be a straight man
but too unsure for the instalment plan,
see, when it comes to male interest
it just profoundly lacks,
and women are just such artefacts.
But then, life's too long
and all too short when I'm
temporarily holding down this fort,
and it's not all that inspiring
and it doesn't even require me.

THAT'S A LOT TO PROCESS

The best way to think of myself is
on a mystical journey
into enlightenment, making amends.
The worst is an uptight, egotistical
bitch who finds it hard to hold friends.
Think of me as a social experiment,
two parents praise their kid
to see how far she gets.
Growing up could be disappointing
and now projection rises
and people fail to surprise me.
But I need all that spiritual connection
buying happiness at the cost of addiction,
been using a pipe like it's a fight
smoking up a teaspoon a day
keeps the distraction away.
keeps the doctor away.
Giving myself those cold showers
Wim Hoff breathing techniques
for all the more powers.
Most times I don't like my body
but other times I think I should
because the skin is just a coating
for everything I'm promoting
and self-love's the new trend
and I'm trying to be trendy
to get a new friend
Can you be addicted to love
with a tendency to be psychotic?
Inflicted by feeling too much,
craving that attention erotic.
Say I'm not a romantic but
I'll tend to trip into love
I try to land it
the first time we meet,
show me some attraction,
eye contact and it's a beat

then I react, I'm obsessed,
checking all your tweets.
Balancing up that only child syndrome
forget I have two brothers part of the kit
Bear in mind, I'm that privileged shit,
all problems too small for it to really hit home,
to really *get* it.
Maybe I'm a better person when I smoke weed
sober, I already miss my mother
because time feels obsolete,
Feeling my daughters' loss of me
and that's just an unrealistic retreat.
I guess I just feel everything a bit
too existentially,
Is it avoidance? Probably not intentionally.
Does anyone else crave sex as much as I do?
No?
Oh yep, I see one hand in the back there.
I think being a cyclist would help me;
a good self-image and some fitness time
but then again, I'm too scared of dying.
Shit. But it's all infinite,
that's what I keep telling myself,
so life can feel more intimate.

Oh, and I'm eating gluten again.

I know I'm thinking about myself too much,
maybe that's the real problem.

So yeah,

that's me.

Thanks for having me.

    flush

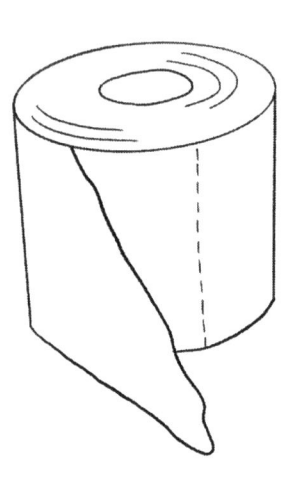

ELIZA PITKIN

You're as sweet as honey, just like my lemon curd,
What I want to do to you,
my favourite f-word.

- Rain -
I learned so much from you,
I hated myself so much because of you,
I've grown so much since you left,
perhaps it was because you left.

~~Either way,~~
~~I wish you could see me now.~~

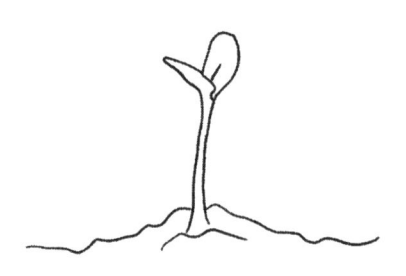

Are you searching or healing?*

(*Suggestion: Mind map your answers and date it)

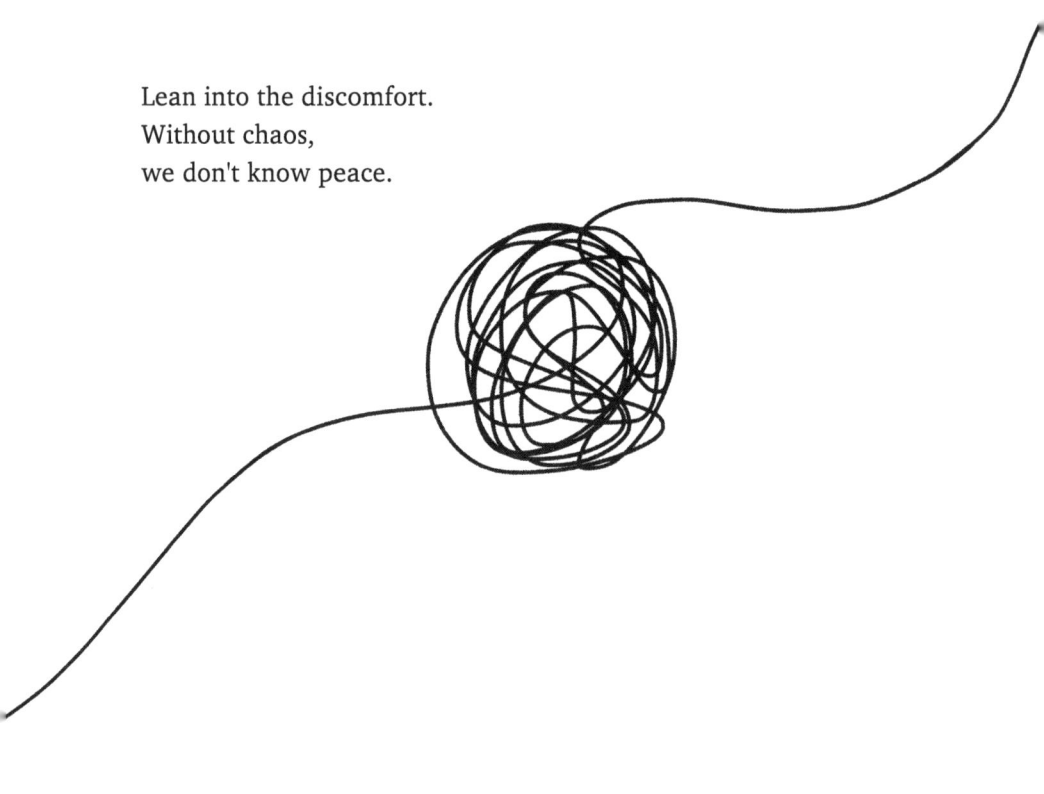

Lean into the discomfort.
Without chaos,
we don't know peace.

- Dating -

But wait,
Are you waiting for gaps
so you can check your apps?
Do I lead you to the pool of thought,
Led you to answers from my own self-taught?
Your old ideas left at circle line eastbound
where you use my ears as a resting ground
for you to spill revelation after revelation,
like some kind of egotistical masturbation
all over my face.
Another lost case.

Or perhaps you're one of the greats,
gripped by the way my upper lip articulates,
unravelling conversation led by organic intuition
as we enter an exchange of ethereal recognition.

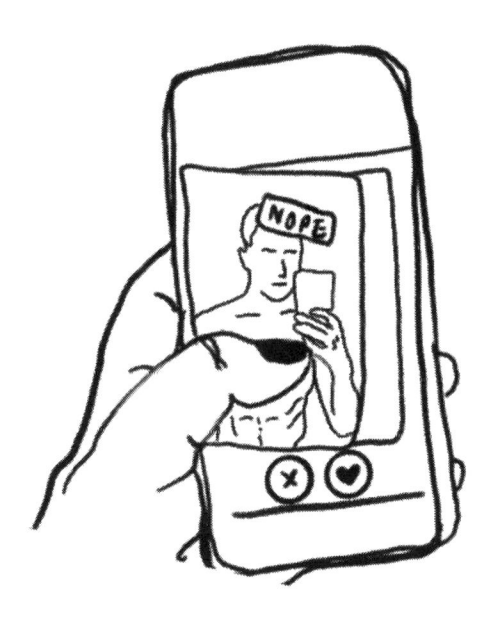

THAT'S A LOT TO PROCESS

I think about it all the time
someone said I mention it in every line.
This barista at costa made milk froth,
caught Fred from work rinsing a cloth,
It made me think about old times,
of all lovers in their primes.
Daydreaming how we met,
how our bodies made duets.
The feeling makes me flushed
Everyday day I'm so blushed,
It's all too much, my cheeks go red.
Broke my cherry in a broken bed.
I love it when you stop and think
I admit I watch you drink
silence, let me lip-sync
like you're saying words dirty.
The idea of something in your mouth
makes me all flirty
(Wait! Concentrate, they're talking.)
I know everything from the way
you're walking
your swing and
your swagger
says you're bragging
or the way you listen
tells me how
we could be kissin'.
See, I like the tomboys,
machismo-psychopaths, cowboys,
boys with toys and tantric-gods,
next door's boy and dad-bods all the
yogis, enlightened chaps intellectuals
and their ego-traps step-dads,
friend's dads, fuckboys,
tight-topped abs,
the vegan lads,

bankers and wankers,
Instagram singers, their talented fingers,
thick bodies and frizzy-haired honeys
fall in love with the women who're funny
that momma and her kids or my old sub teacher
the masculine girl and the guy with the soft features,
friends brothers, their sisters
self-assured hipsters,
the guy on the tube,
ex's brother dude, the stoner dudes,
gym girls and their mirror selfies
red-heads, brunettes and bright blondes
all that soft skin and girls with their glasses
The empathic lover and the full-on narcissists
wobbly bodies and fresh-faced ladies
to all the women who praise me
girls on the night out, cuties in bagginess
big ones, small ones, and so-called 'saggy'-ness
Of course, all introverted naturals when we meet
and long-skirt wearing hippies and their beautiful feet
it goes on,

and you're definitely in there.

*"Energy cannot be created or destroyed,
it can only be changed from one form to another"* - **Albert Einstein**

    you are energy

    so when you die

    what happens to that energy?

I've been told to soften
it's 'cause
I'm too high too often
a dual reality:

        my own split personality

I thought to myself;

   No one can see me right now

      Am I crossing anyone's mind right now?

         Is my name being written down somewhere?

           There are gaps where

              no one is thinking of me.

                 In those gaps, I thought to myself,

                        How do I exist?

- Sacred Geometry -

I believe it's important to believe in something.
But it's less about believing and more about seeing.
Why are we here? What purpose do we serve? What's the point?
I look to what's here for meaning, other creations other than me.
This life is physical, tangible, in front of you.
It's about looking beyond the basic form.
We need to be brought into the physical form
to be perceived, noticed, heard.
What is it that animates your physical form?
Is it the breathing?
The intangible, conscious illusion that moves through you?
Everything owns it's own uniqueness
Whilst following the guidelines of symmetry, of a group.
The physical is textural.
whether it's gooey, furry, wet, shiny, porous, soft or a shell,
and it's full of colour that flickers and fractals with light,
aroma's, taste, temperature. It ages.
From nothing, to seed, to raw, to fruit, to wrinkled, to rot, to seed.
Patterns, the mathematics of sacred geometry.
Communicate to me, to us, they say, nothing is random.
Everything is as it should be.
You are a part of this geometry.
I believe that the body is way of communicating.
like the fruit, we're full of seeds.
Seeds of ideas, truth, experience, love, connections.
This reoccurring theme that is infinite, choreographed,
created without words.
Just look at something.
Take away its randomly assigned name, the memories around it,
a connotation, a like or dislike. See it for what it is. Just sense it.
Recognise your self within it.

And now, look at yourself in this way.

ELIZA PITKIN

just came online

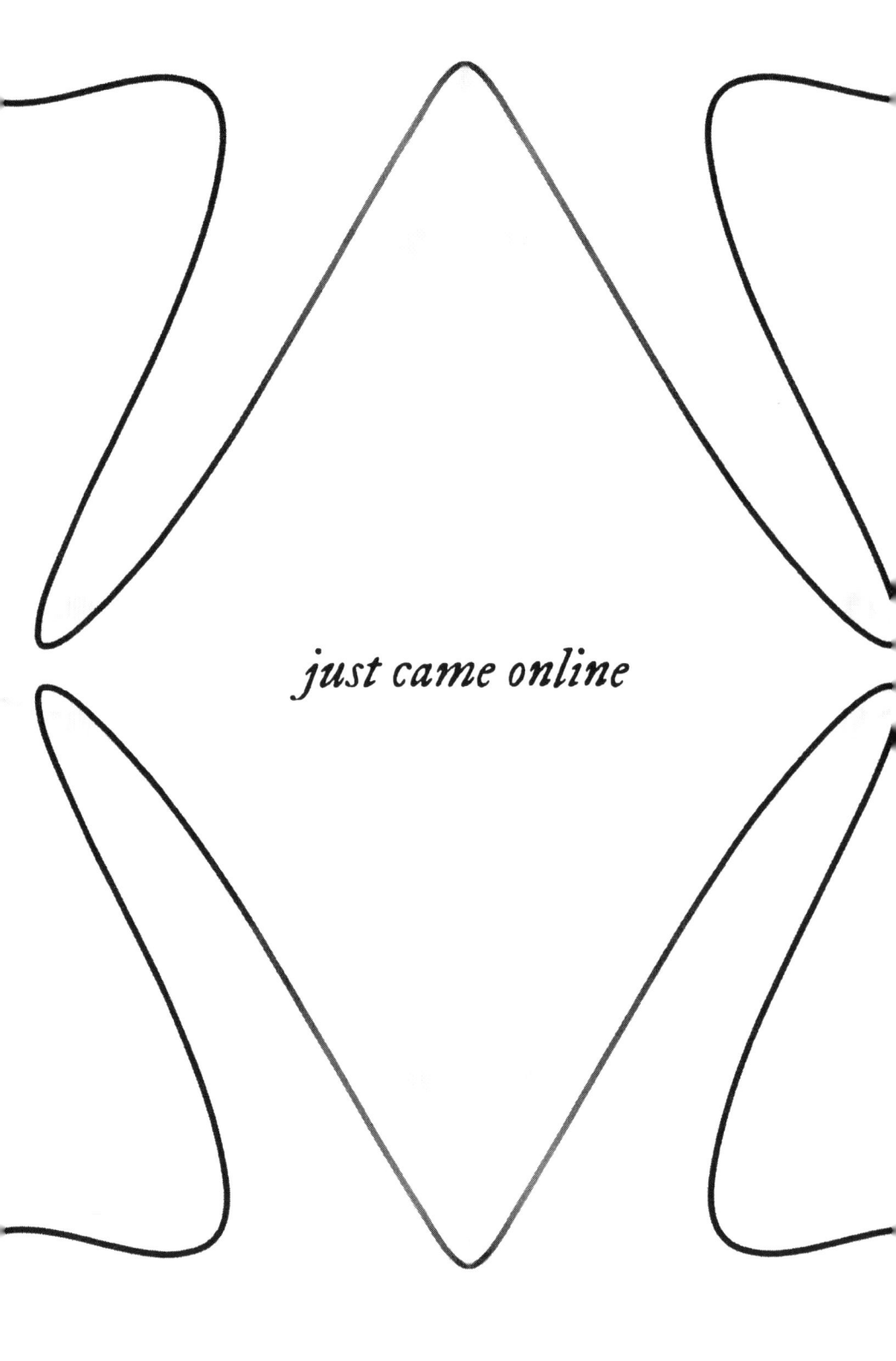

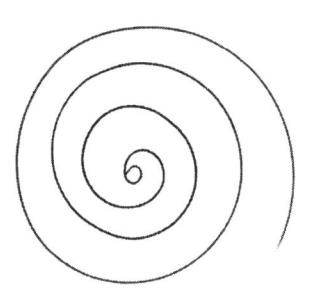

This next spurt is dreamy, nostalgic, all of those secret thoughts that stir around in our heads when we're alone. I describe the more angsty sides of my isolated experience. This is emphasised through dream worlds, routines, memories, addictions and where I see myself reflected in the bigger world. Reading it back I feel a sense of loss and what could've been. I cannot state a specific time in my life that I wrote these, as it is more of a subconscious narrative, like all the invisible thoughts and dreams that have no specific relationship to our physical reality. This is my own secret state of living (now not so secret).

If I was going to put colours or texture to this chapter I would give it purples, blacks, neon orange and metal textures. If it was a taste it would be a strong one, like bitter lemon or whisky.

- Teenage Oppression/Obsession -

Listen,
as she reminisces
treading through wet grass
like her guidance is missing
lips like she's kissing
heartbeat too fast,
from cut glass,
watching her sip slow
mouth of ocean flood-like
sipping blood-like sloe gin
her whole soul
scrunched up
with a safety pin.
        Knuckles print red marks
        from precocious ring parts
        from her hand holding me tightly
        through this simulation,
        games, so sightly
        my 'cute' admiration
        titillating   temptation
        invigorating   sensation as
        her cold fingers taking a toke
        watching her, and all this thick smoke.
                Life with her is all my icky come-downs,
                and every little thing that makes soft sounds
                a tease she can be for how free she can make me feel,
                glowing sticky sponge stuck to a spoon
                growing pains crammed in one bedroom.
                Sickly smells of our pheromones
                and sweet treacle undertones
                        With dilated eyes tightly knit,
                        I know I'm addicted to all of it:
                        Playing parts in our fantasies
                        incarnated,
                        life between child and adult
                        is birth reincarnated
                        all my teenage oppression divinely translated

JUST CAME ONLINE

Drugs opened doorways into your mind
welcomed you into rooms you never knew you'd find.
These rooms are like a hotel, windows into the soul.
The fear is closing the doors on what remains reality,
that which maintains the hold.

- Things that hang -

The smell of sugar
in your first lover's car
combined with shampooed hair
draped around shoulders
a quilt half off,
half on.
Like the curtains hanging
in our second house,
Sheets of fabric to block the sun.
We hang skins like that
outside shops.
Eat bananas
we drink from things that hang
like the udders of unhappy cows
or dripping honey from hives.

Dreamcatchers hang over my bed
like the earphones hanging from my head.
A pendulum swinging,
the screeching sound
of the school bell ringing.
It reminds me of the first
genitals I saw
feeling its own air,
it was a man without a care.

We hang up images
as to not forget
like portals of memory
hung up on walls,
mirrors are for now
disco lights are for school balls.
Stuck in nostalgia like wind chimes
in my mother's greenhouse.

The stench of a joint that
sits in the air
something unseen but feels shared,
like answers left unsaid
a phone off its hook,
silence
a book slips
a rope rips,
laundry dancing.

Sometimes I carry the memory of last night's dream.

It kind of stays with me like glitches of a memory
Find myself craving the stitches my mind sends me.
There's not enough meaning when it's hard to find,
all I know is that it's another life I've left behind.

"It was only a dream"

Sometimes I wonder,
What does the dream realm call *this reality?*

- Life as a Sim -

The memory distorter of childhood n' school.
My life as a sim stranded in the pool,
pleasure belongs to the family of tentacles,
self-asphyxiation of a head under-water.
Hold your breath test for self-will slaughter,
Tongue taste of chlorine and the smell of feet,
keeping head above board, wait for the drought
'cause some sick trick pulled the ladder out,
I'm told.
I took a breath and now I'm old,
wrap my head 'round a spell.
In so many ways I am mould
because I just cannot tell,
if I am screaming in this reality
or swimming through endless mortality.

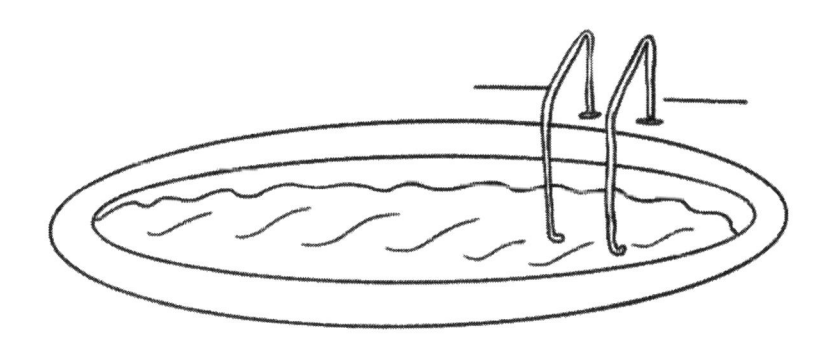

- Dream Being -

It's all since I came off that smoke
Now dream state is what it provokes.
I leave leaves soaking until I pour mugwort,
Mix it with a mug keeping that cacao raw.
A ritual for the subconscious to allow the dream being,
all neurosis, self-diagnosis, and all those true feelings.
I've been studying this avatar for a while,
here's to you, my dream self, drippy and shy.
The school corridors are the haunted maze
soaking memories through this foggy haze.
Old and familiar faces play parts, playing it cool
amongst passing time pulsing the folding walls.
Sexual desires manifest without consent,
my soul pulling strings for me to see itself.
Doorways are too short, unreachable shelves,
the toilets are a murky black, a sight of grime,
for this floating observer, a rabbit running from time.
All this time I've spent searching and checking maps
for too many things to carry and too many traps.
It's all those things I miss, memories in an abyss.
I can feel eyes watching me from the floors,
all my flaws, fears, and desires
and the leering inquiries
that it's caused.

JUST CAME ONLINE

- My Biggest Fan -

He smells my scent like I'm on heat,
catches my heels with his feet
until he trips me up and clamps me with his teeth,
folds his elbows in a beat, holding me beneath.
He's breathy and warm,
seconds count before my clothes are torn.
He takes me in all senses but the eyes,
keeps them shut whilst pinching my thighs.
Like a dance of intuition, everything in the now
this animal behind my body, waiting for him to allow
me to spin me 'round to face his hardened skin
he holds my jaw and withholds kisses on my chin.
He's primitive and tender, my biggest fan,
he would chase me 'round the flat if I ran.
His fingers are like decorations on my body, adorning,
breathes me in like I'm air in the morning
I'm Aphrodite, the goddess herself,
shining and wise like pushing books in a shelf,
He pushes and pokes and draws swirls
with his fingertips like pearls
summoning beads of sweat
that cover me with gems to beset
my knotted hair like a jewelled rope
and all this wetness as his soap
he plays me like a creature,
my mouth is his 'breather'
a break between the race
between my thighs to my navel,
the dare to beat his last time
he made me come in my prime
Replaying all his last records
So he pleasures me for rewards
I'm instrumental with keys and chords
strings to pluck, an aura to fuck
until I scream and roar,
He'll stroke me soft and sore.
I taste like melon and lime he said,
as if copper was a syrup instead.

ELIZA PITKIN

'evolution is an adaptation to one's environment for survival'

Yet, humans have destroyed their environment,
not adapted to it.
Explore this idea with me:

Perhaps we're wired wrong,
or maybe we're not an animal at all?
Maybe we're more like fungi.
In more ways, we are like mould,
the unwanted sprouts covering mother earth.
Overpopulation, feeding off all the worlds resources,
Living off gluten, dead animals, and sugar,
like the fur that lives of decomposing bodies.
We absorb all the nutrients and resources of the Earth.
If we are more like bad bacteria,
then it's in our nature to take captivity
of ourselves, each other, animals,
our bodies and our environment.

Imagine if we were the parasite invading our world.

Can we evolve without destruction?

- Time -

don't you like the way I'm circulating
I'm not trying to be too dominating,
see it more as a motivation
in some numerical formation.
To help create some sense of order
for you to create activity with a border,
these capture a directory of experience
and calls them memories,
makes me feel a difference.
You're feeling me all intuitively
looking how we age each other
cycling around but moves life forward
I'm mathematical and circular but towards
linear and repetitive, frightfully insensitive,
but spiritual by nature, a force unruled.
Even if clocks were all broken,
it's a mere sense as a token.
The moon and sun will rise a new day
as I'm here moving moments away.
It is life happening to us,
here to inhabit us.

JUST CAME ONLINE

-Dear-

I'm so flattered
so here's all my heart,
sorry it's so battered.
Squeeze it tight in the palm of Your hand
Beats like a drum when in holy land
My whole body under your thumb
like crumbs under the carpet.
For You are the thing underthings
like all the pink under my skin.
I watch you on tele with the candlelit,
Your open-mouth kisses I can't handle it
Enclosed is a lock of my hair
and some rosey red underwear,
wrap it 'round Your little finger,
Committed, I linger.
Also a glass of my scent infused.
I watched all your past interviews
My love for you is no passing fad,
You and I both are two nomads,
They say you're mad but
You're just a nihilist.
Open-mouth kisser,
A sweet listener.
Here is all of me
all to Yourself,
here's my letter
so you know
I know you,
better
than
you.

ELIZA PITKIN

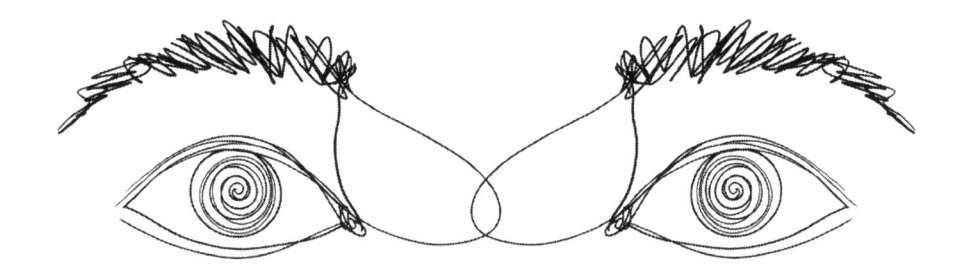

(you're the only person in the world that's seen life through your eyes)

- self-declaration -

I refuse to 'accept all'
to have my mouth
stuffed with cookies
so I can be a piece
of data for people
who seek to
dominate us.

I refuse to shave my body hair
because an unsaid rule mindlessly
continues to prefer
the look of under-developed bodies.

I refuse to
watch videos and shows
of people desperately
seeking recognition,
to later buy something
from one of those people
because
they came up
whilst I scrolled,
to benefit the pockets of
those who pursue money
as their life's currency.

In a nutshell,
I refuse to be asleep
when there's infinity
to be awake for.

Can anyone understand my diction?
I keep craving for some kind of perfection,

      I'm just wanting some of that connection;
            not wifi, *I'm high*
              just a fraction of affection.
           A struggle with reality, bad attraction,

              so I take on a personality,

                  it's a tragedy.

You've been gifted with life,
But it's given with a fine
Can't avoid death and tax
Unravelling fiction from facts,
Spending your life, thinking;
Where is it in this twisted soul of mine?
Itched by the wondering
of whether this is
a simulated reality,
I ask myself,
is this all real or just a fallacy?
But I play the game;
Take my name
and play like
I was born to play the role
Doing it with class, like I do
with my legs wrapped round a pole
The show must go on, but
I call myself Truman
Rinsing the tears
from the burdens I didn't choose;
The blue of my bruises
The pips in my teeth
And all that I call being human,
Included with all the childhood wounds
that's what we found,
The memories are them are all
that's left for you now.
That and a thorny wreath
Curling 'round your head

Take me from the land of thieves to which I was led
Would you blow on the food I'm fed?
Before you leave, would you tuck me up in bed?

fly me to the place where geometric shapes mean love
where my parallel universe does reside
peel back all the layers that make up my reality and
show me the colours of the multiverse
remind me that I'm part of something bigger
show me the feeling of the power that holds us all

- Aegosexual -

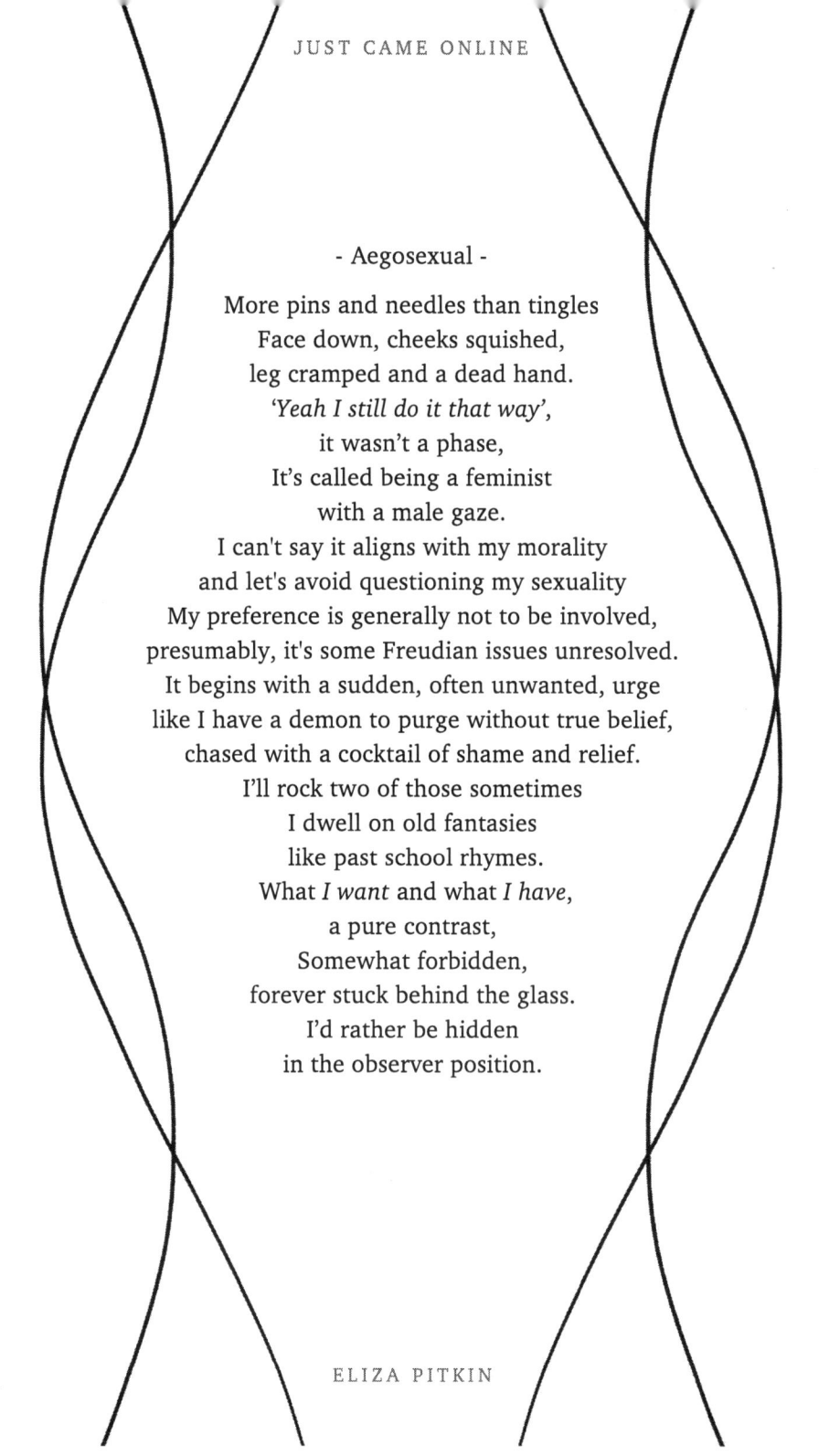

More pins and needles than tingles
Face down, cheeks squished,
leg cramped and a dead hand.
'Yeah I still do it that way',
it wasn't a phase,
It's called being a feminist
with a male gaze.
I can't say it aligns with my morality
and let's avoid questioning my sexuality
My preference is generally not to be involved,
presumably, it's some Freudian issues unresolved.
It begins with a sudden, often unwanted, urge
like I have a demon to purge without true belief,
chased with a cocktail of shame and relief.
I'll rock two of those sometimes
I dwell on old fantasies
like past school rhymes.
What *I want* and what *I have*,
a pure contrast,
Somewhat forbidden,
forever stuck behind the glass.
I'd rather be hidden
in the observer position.

- Disgusted -

When they mention it to me, see
how my hairs stand on end
like my fingers got the blend,
spinning silver blades as
the memory of them fades.
The whole thing is repulsive.
Now I react with impulsion,
Their consideration is lagging
obvious like the dog's breath wagging
in my face
or the taste
between a woman's thighs, bitter like
his rewritten lies,
I can handle her 'little girl act'
her issues erasing the fact that our
dirty washing is still soaking and it's
all just too broken
like the glass I smashed
"she always lashes out
just to see how they
react;"
But it's all okay,
my hand is still intact.

JUST CAME ONLINE

If I had multiple lives
I would spend the next one with you,

I just need to see what I can do.

I love so much about you,
like you're so full of spaces
pauses shown in your personality
causes unknown bits about you
like the gaps
between your fingers
and under
your pits and
and hesitant lips
The gap between my hips;
and all the air
between your hair,
like the lingering
between your
messages,
and all the rest of it.
Please don't
be a friend,
leave me enough
of your spaces
so I can pretend
they're filled
with things
I love about
you,
it's a shield,
with so few sides
of you elected,
just the
small bits I've
selected.
Like a mirror,
you're my reflected
all my desires for a partner
projected.

- Plant -

Is it wrong that
I just popped a chong?
I'm not an addict or anything
I'm just a real fanatic about it
Lips to the pipe like I'm on automatic.
My body goes all gooey,
Now in tune with Feng Shui
I know what doors to close,
which windows to crack
burn incense for my nose
and pull the heavy curtains back.
It's a real sense that life's all cathartic,
made me circle the borders of my garden,
took photographs of block colours in nature
To animals and all little creations,
you and I haven't spoken for a while.
Wanting to mix it up for a try so
I pinch some cinnamon in my coffee
and then write my heart out in a hurry.
Suddenly feel a flush of ideas, it's all clever
when it becomes a spiritual endeavour
all activity is what meditation is caressing
it's cooking, running, talking, resting
listening, singing and creating.
It's like I get it now, it's just reframing
Now, doing it every day it seems,
Man, life is like one long dream
Last night's hit is like today's,
it's an ongoing stream.
A calm sense of my own fate
I was nicer to my roommate,
the weather, oh how glorious your energy is

How stunning the colour scheme fits
Everything is an art form, a kind of meditation
This moment is an occasion,
it's all patience, elation and creation,
whilst I'm all intoxicated.
My ears make bonds with my conscious
I hear all the things that make more sense
Everything is funny, it's not so tense.
Feeling enough company for one,
I change up my hairstyle for some fun
there's just no real tension when
I'm locked into this dimension
and sadly I like this more than 'reality,'
the usual just feels like a formality.
I don't need anyone in this life.
I can feel more myself and it's alright
I just hate it when it starts fading,
but in this moment I'm elated.

Show me why we're connected,
give me some meaning
So I know everything about you is for the keeping
Moon gazing as we gaze at what's above us
Boo, blaze with me and talk like we're old lovers,
Let's snuggle up under the fort of our auras
Tell me where it started, map out your traumas
I want to tell you what has torn me up
Come up here baby, this is just a warm up
I want you to really see me,
So sweetie speak to me freely
like your conscience is spilling through you
Filling in the clues
let's pretend it's 2am,
we've had one too many drinks
and you don't care what I think
Let go of any self-image you want to mould
talk to me like we're over a hundred years old
Honey, be my life support system
Fill me up with all your wisdom

Your body moves to your language, so pure

Your soul dancing in front of me, it's allure

Characterising itself through the human form

I want to hear all of you, stripped bare and raw.

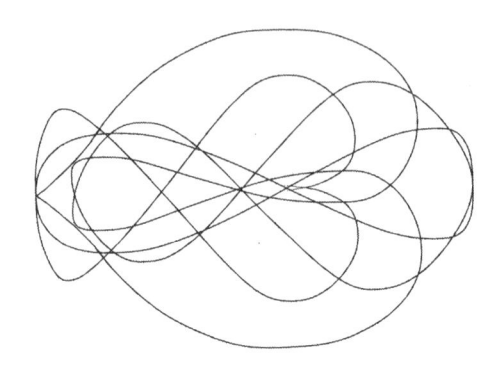

when you love each other to bits
but you know you're not *the one*

those are the often the most beautiful and breathtaking
chapters of one's life

- Losing Grip -

The whole thing is some sinking feeling,
what I now see as divine consciousness was
once demons mouths like burnt holes in my ceiling,
wondering if it's healing when the paint chips start peeling.
I can't remember if that was the effect of the diazepam,
or the reason I was taking it.
It left blotches in my eyes as the light flashed,
this morning a coffee cup cracked
bled boiling water poured through finger gaps
I ran to the sink, and then ran the tap, "sigh"
grabbed the towel, too late I was bone dry.
I dreamt that night my ears burst blood from high volume
it plugged me back in the room,
plunged straight from the womb.
Trapped myself in my own coop
Repeating myself like I'm on a loop
Take me to the edge to make me
appreciate my sanity as a stable reality.

When you feel empty,
remember,
you are not empty.

You are the vast space
looking around at it's own shell.

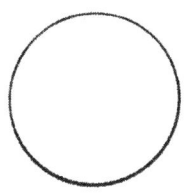

Now, you're the thing holding that shell.

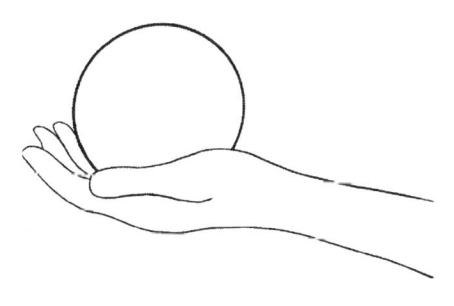

- Loading -

To 'be' in the body;
is to react,
observe and
interact.
Then there's a sudden jolt
and the world feels outside of you again.

This is the updating process.

During this time
it's best to look at life objectively.
Let it load.
In need of some bug fixes.
Click a few things,
correct some things here and there,
activate a higher level of playfulness,
a perspective shift,
a new coding system,
a comfort in old anxieties.
Nearly done.
Complete,
and you're back into the body.

This is how we grow,
it's just some people never update.

(just to update you)

to live harmoniously
we all need to update ourselves
but we all need the same coding to begin again

~~how are you?~~

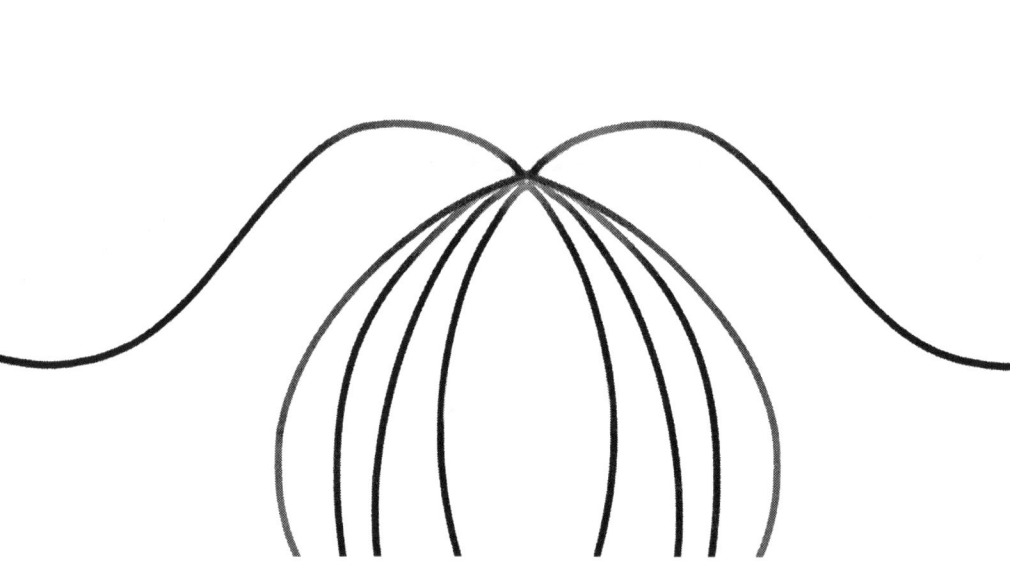

hope you're well

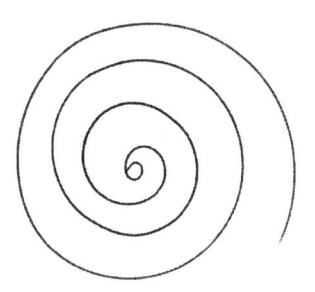

This spurt was originally called 'Letters to the chamber.' These are unsent letters to the people in my life, conceptual/made-up characters within society, and parts of myself. The process of writing unsent letters can be a powerful experience for soothing the mind of all of its unsaid things. It helped me understand more of what makes me who I am. It felt objective, but ultimately loving at its core.

Please do this, that is to write to anyone (including yourself). Perhaps someone you think about often, or something you wish you could tell that person. The act of acknowledging how we feel is frequently more powerful than having those people hear it. You can reveal a lot to yourself.

Open it by describing them, then your experience with them, thank them for things, forgive them for things, and wish good things for them.

Surprise yourself.

With this one, I imagine the consistency of gum, but runnier, like a melted marshmallow. The colours are earthy light browns with sparkles.

Dear future self,

please don't talk shit about me

I'm doing the best I can
with the time
and knowledge
I have.

Love,
present self

p.s. look forward to being u

- When the milk separates -

and then I see the almond milk that curdled in my tea
and it made me realise how many hurdles feel unreal.
It makes me crazy how much I adapt
like this exercise is taking on daily crap.
You'll know where I've walked,
I'm a creating path of scrap paper
so sick of my own laugh,
stepped in my own dirty knickers,
it's shameful.
Life's like a tickle when it gets painful
with new sex tricks that are just shoddy
'cause I choose biscuits over my "old" body.
Old memories of regrets lay in the fabric of my bed,
all the strange things I've said creep as I fall asleep
and the distraction is just lousy, it's pure arousal
to make it make-believe, to allure in pure fantasy,
fake it, make myself believe the times were real.
I'm angry at all the fragile egos and false facades
walking around with backbones made of glass
an ordeal, faking my own apologies, I don't care.
I can smell old bong water that hangs in the air.
Why can't my ideas be the ones they all love?
We're all run by fear that's why there's such a rush,
Mind you, I can't say I like my new friend very much.
I don't like my body but would prefer to be naked
but my feet are ripped because the doc martens are breaking.
It's just two days later and eyebrow hairs begin to show
like little black fly legs beginning to grow
out my face and hang above my eyes
maybe one for each cry, or all the lies
or all the naughty lust,
collecting thoughts like dust,
except I don't clean the shelves enough.

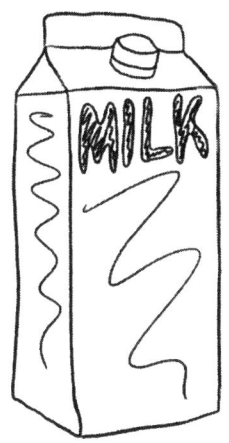

middle of a sentence

(Hand up)

"Sorry excuse me, hi

Can I ask you something?
Thank you
Um
..are you capable of not interrupting?
I was literally just creating sonic magic from my mouth...
and then you suddenly you started speaking.

No, but are you capable of not interrupting?
It's just a question, are you -- ?
Yup, great! Well then, would you mind exercising that when I'm talking, please?
No, I'm actually asking, would you mind?
Yeah?
You feel you can do that?
You're capable of doing that?
...You never know, I might say something interesting, you may...dare I say it... learn something.

Lovely!

So, as I was saying..."

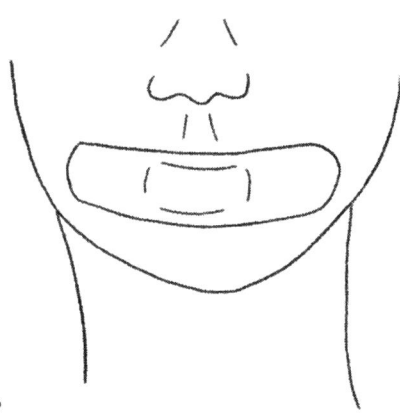

We all came out the same womb,
Maybe it's about finding a whole new group.
Maybe it's human nature for siblings to part.
Yeah, like seeds scatter to find a new start.

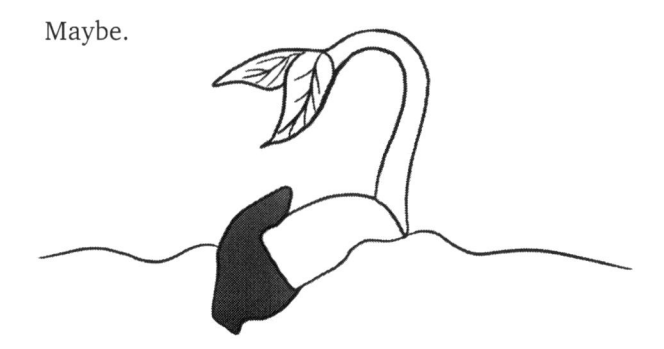

Maybe.

- Mermaid -

So if there is another power at play
then I'm glad they put us together.
To say how it feels to have a friend
before I was even born,
a union was spawn to guide and sync up,
To grow and watch over and relinquish
Through your souls texture of sunflower petals
with melodic notes in soulful tones to settle us
underneath the heavy quilt we hide under
we both were escaping different things
through our play.
Can't you see her diamond blue eyes
and her laughing face that's too shiny
Looking back I see that your feelings hurt
Resting in the hems of our beating hearts
I run my hand passed the walls
hearing the sounds of our childhood rules.
You're made of loving, you really are something.
Your scales are your badges sewn into your skin,
it's yours and it's shapeshifting.
I'm here I'm being, I'm listening
with all my heart and openness,
tell me what you need the mostest.

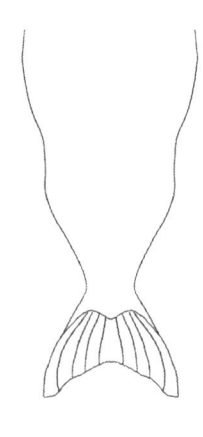

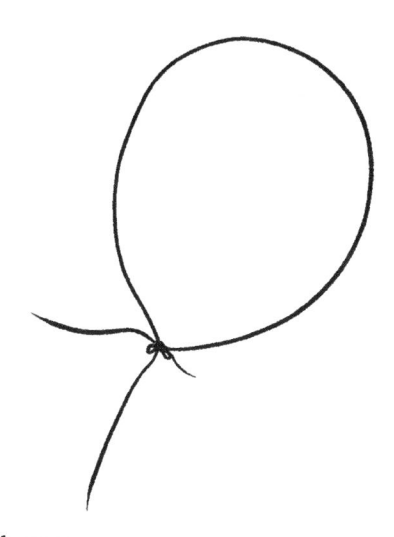

But my love, I didn't break up with you.
I broke up with the person you choose to become.
I can't compete with a promise you can't keep.

one lives in the past,
the other in the future

and no one's here

                (with me)

to all the thoughts I shouldn't be having

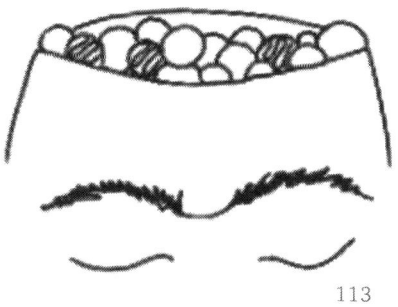

- Soul Sister -

her mother
a symbol of womanhood
a sister by soul
a hand through this life
she's earth and gems
aloof and elegant
an open wound
she's all the lessons
and heartbreak,
the most naturally
playful and sweetest
person that glows.
A river of trust
and inspiration
that flows.

She plays hide and seek with her inner child,
Ageing left shame and guilt all stored and filed
Rummaging through the fears pushed in a pile.
Scraping her hands on her brothers clutter
Past words, lies and resentment now a mutter
She salts out the words left in her wounds
As she rinses the cloth of her mother's feuds
Replacing these bandages with facts
and lacing boundaries with crusty scabs

I had to get away from it, life, I choose it
Waking up in this life, I choose to go lucid

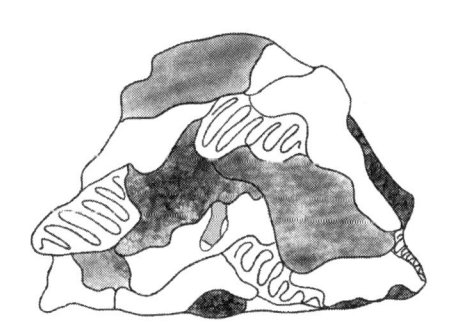

- That's a bit deep for the dinner table -

It's a
kind of a reaction
to the frail existence
that we stand on.
Why are we here?

We're attracted to ignorance,
we lack. It's lies, and violence.
I'm here, I'm being, I'm breathing
but they don't seem to be ing,
or hear me thinking, *What's it all for?*
Because I can't always see the floor,
It's lovely and all that,
until it's a bit of a bore,
a discourse and disconnection
remains the constant sore,
I stick for the love and affection
but surely there's a kind place somewhere,
but it's unfair,
that love and divine consciousness is {out there}
The pain and gain of life is a growing cancer,
when the question of *"why"* is too big to answer.

Combined with the voice inside my head that keeps talking
it's narrating and frustrating, kind and insulting
but that's only if I look there,
because over there it's too dark
it's a greasy, sticky trapped lair,
a release of my body to the shark;
Their ads, their fads, and false facades,
Teasing our triggers and deepest scars.
This is all that confusion bumbled into one
it's scary, strange and far too rough.

We're all in that confusion,
please don't let it be a delusion.
Let's not live for the next space launch
or a glimpse of a thigh from girls who flaunt,
or that package you want that's currently in transit,
If you're not asking the question
of what's the point and why're we all here?
Then you're living with ignorance and fear,
you'll never sit in that difficult place
it's magical and starry abyss to face,
endless learning of queries
it's unravelling, day-dreamy
otherwise you're far too sleepy
in your head and that's just creepy.

Hold hands with mothers, lovers and listen,
hold each other in confusion and bliss.

When we look the other way, an ego creates
that discriminates, dominates and eradicates
the peaceful confusion that sits and awaits.

Trust me, it's a journey un-turning but it's worth it,

"you're worth it."

'You're being attacking"

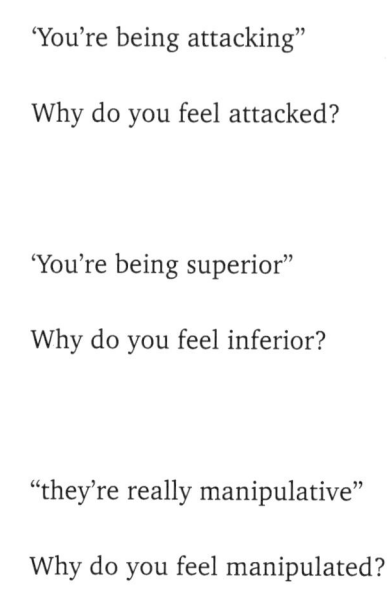

Why do you feel attacked?

'You're being superior"

Why do you feel inferior?

"they're really manipulative"

Why do you feel manipulated?

- Let's talk about why -

Empathy
/ˈɛmpəθi/

(noun)

the ability to understand and share the feelings of another.

Do you have this?

(Yeah, but do you *really*?)

Imagine if everyone had empathy,
What would that look like?

Angel

I do think there are angels
I'm not sure how or why
but they're kind
and patient,
and
beautiful innately
and in every way.

so, forget the words coming out of their mouth,
they're not helpful

Let's find out what they *really mean,*
what are they saying?
What's the intention
underneath everything?
What are they saying about them self?
Are they afraid of something?
Maybe they want something?

What's the intention under that?

(Let's get even deeper.)

Underneath everything
you'll find that
gooey human bit

and right there,
that's where you are.

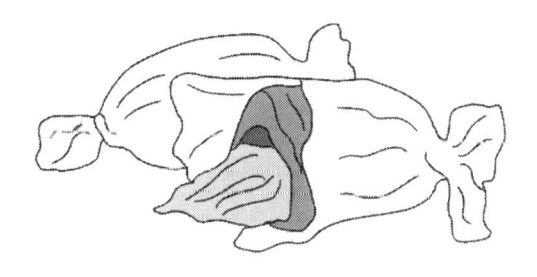

- passing feeling -

and every now and then a flaming feeling sits inside
my head,
it's legs residing in my stomach.

'Maybe it's me'

Was I horrible?
Did I block myself off?
Am I just a bit odd?

It would make sense,
'that's *so* me.'

(and then the feeling passes and I'm back to being okay with myself again)

I could see humans being lost in translation
I spent most of my childhood facilitating
a narration
between parents in conflict
with lack of emotional confidence.
It became my own little power.

The power is wise,
it's instinct when it rises.

*Thank you to me
for creating that tool,
it served me well for
all these years
but for now,
it's no longer useful.*

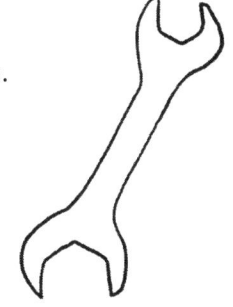

(*what's your tool?)

we're so clever
we're so obviously superior
because we have language
and thought

we're inventors, explorers,
artists and politicians, attention-seekers,
border controllers,
ego- centric and power-happy
we invented the wheel
for cars and then planes
now we can fly
with the expense of pollution
we make bombs and nuclear gasses.
But we're not all the same
we have men and women
Men are born hunters
so we trap animals
bleed them dry and hang them up
Women are just better at home making
and sweet treat baking.
We know there's pain and poverty
in the same way we know there
are rich folk in pedophile rings,
see, we're sexual beings,
it's in our nature and
we just love green paper.
Not bad for us cavemen,
us apes on shrooms
we make robots and tools.
We invented the internet

for 5 second commercials
to see tits and girls
with unclean mouths.
We're profile pictures,
bundles of bios,
another version of ourselves.
We make sugar for children
and cocaine for the grown ups,
snort it up with 20 quid note.

        we're so clever
        we're so obviously superior
        because we have language
        and thought

HOPE YOU'RE WELL

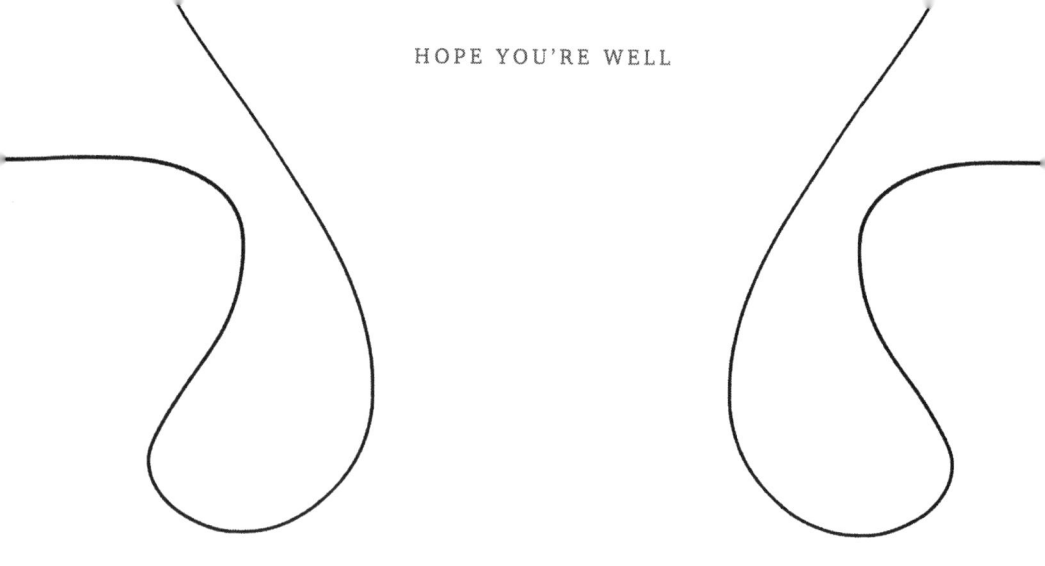

- Happy you exist -

You taught me what love looks like
that it exists and can be gained and grown
You're gentle, and conscious in all the nice places
Thank you for extending yourself through a family
Thank you for being a life-long friend

- please like me again -

Do I have to say, 'I didn't mean that,'
say I'm sorry for all my feedback?
Maybe it was character assassination
but I kept trying to be creative.
The rocky grain of your doorstep is
stuck to my knees,
it's beginning to sting like
your post box hole
printed in my forehead skin.
Please let me in,
I'll be way less intense,
just help me to pretend
I'm not more than enough
but instead,
I'm all the things above.

i've been thinking

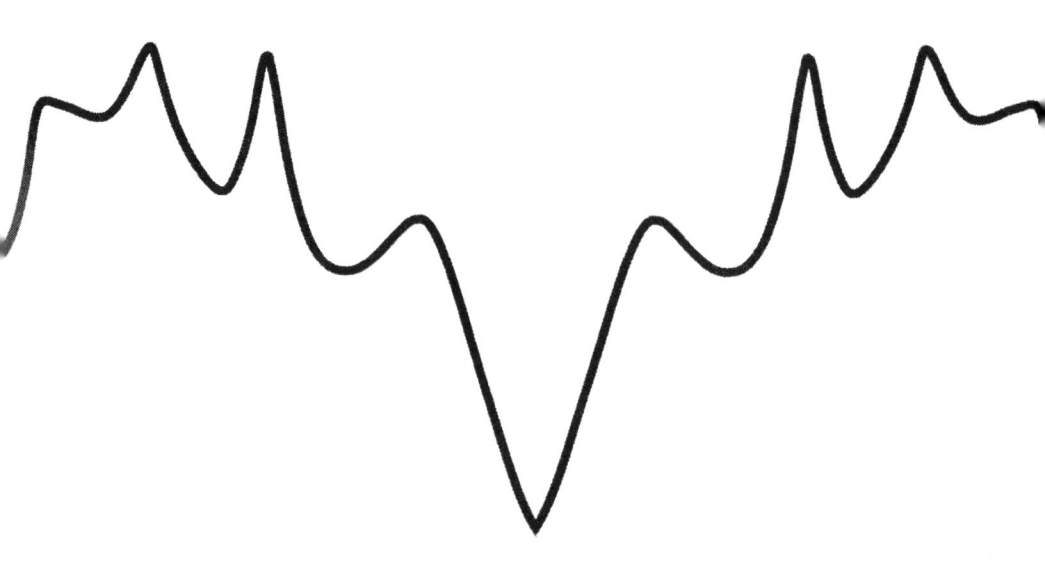

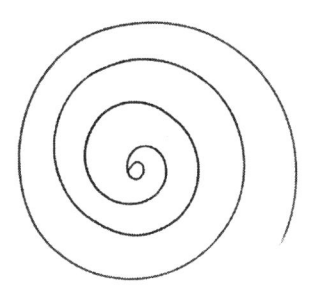

This next spurt feels like an examination of the culture around me. The world of untethered humans amidst ego-driven conditioning, the digital abyss of social media, the increasing disillusionment of politics, the passing strangers plugged into podcasts, exposed social disparities, and the anticipation of an unprecedented global hibernation. I'm looking at the separations and the unions that are made. What breaks? What comes back stronger? What doesn't feel relevant at all anymore? It's about communicating to those unseen parts of ourselves; looking at our relationship with identity, loss, devotion, justice, heaven and mindfulness all within the contemporary social culture.

Writing this spurt brought up some grief about various parts of my life, and writing those parts helped me to find the empowerment in being human. It consequently allowed me to become softer, more humorous, and more forgiving.

It makes me imagine the feeling of train rides, the texture of velvet, and everything that's blue. I hope there is something in this chapter that feels familiar to you.

Mother Nature,
the less privileged humans in the world,
all the things I'm not addressing,
the mystery of the meaning to life,
all animals,
our history,
past lovers,

I'm sorry. I love you.

Please give me another chance, I'll be better *this* time, I promise.

I got distracted, but I'm listening now.

What were you saying about harmony?

I want to try it.

Love,

(tip)

To be a good love-maker
you have to really tune in;
to your body,
and theirs.

I grieve breakups.

Introduction into life was a little abrupt,
'cause life outside interrupt the love.
In love with my mother, all a precursory
ripped from her hands on the first day of nursery
My parents were ill-matched,
but together they latched
onto underhand comments and tears that were shed,
two opposites slamming mine and their heads.

Then my heart got broken.
That was my first lover,
somewhat a token for
what followed others.

Living a life of
climate ignorance and wars
made by us,
borders made by fascists,
separation and culture clashes.
Turns out,
When there's no love
for the environment,
There's so much violence.

But then perhaps it's fate
that I broke up with my child self,
my real self, my natural state.

There's so much heartbreak along the way,

Maybe 'break up'
is in my DNA.

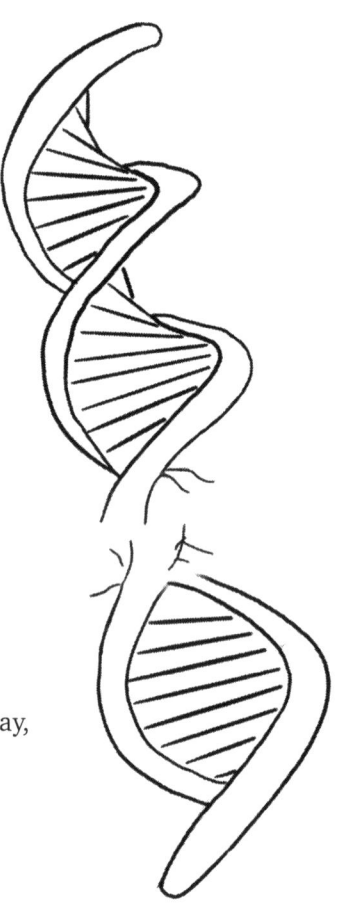

I stubbed my toe on the sofa,
Fuck!
Life, why did you do this to me?

- The moment I self-reflect -

- Commit -

Then they held my hand and said they'd marry me,
the round ring around their eyes beating at mine.

This is it,
this is *that* true love moment.
If this moment is is all we ever have…
Say it.
Say *yes,*
Say,
"I love you,
    yes,
        I do."

But wait, before I do that,

Does love mean the same thing to us?

For example,
I love you with language
like it runs from my mouth,
spilling the feelings of vows,
Like for better or for worse
meaning from every hardship,
we immerse.
I wish to only speak the same language as you,
so not what we say, but *what we mean*
will come through.
We trust that not one of us will drop out,
when energies run high
there's no cop-out.
I could become a worse person if I'm tested,
worked on the soul and became disinterested.
Don't utter words involving "I"
when we're an *'us'*, we both try,
We leave our egos to the side
and allow ourselves to synergise
because I need you

like you need devotion,
I know that's
what you need
it's your insecurity.
See our emotional growth in full motion.
What about in sickness and in health?
Like when the body of my soul needs more help?
Can I depend on you as you could for me?
How about for richer, or for poorer,
loyalty amongst desire and good fortune,
In case the material life pulled you towards her.
What if we were stripped of what identifies us
No money, no career, all that incentivises us,
Is that thing called 'love' still there?
Let's lean into 'let no man put asunder'
So when you scroll at night, you won't wonder
Whether love and legs would be greener
A flirtation of others would make you keener
Let there be no secrets between our sheets
No false projection of me should you believe
I promise to work on myself
So it's fair
so I can work on us,
as a pair.
Learn how I love,
through eyes and celebration,
know that'll we'll grow and re-shape our formation.
I promise I'll always listen with full attention
We, the protector of our best intention.
If you can love me this way, we made a complete
because I value your values, and you're valued to me.
I love your wholeness,
what yours is what's mine
and all that hold us
is our true divine.

{ So, does love mean the same thing to us? }
　　Because if it doesn't perhaps it's just lust.

Dear his mum and dad,

Never mind me,

Just another person to tell you what a *lovely* man your son is.
How did you raise such a *'nice guy'*?

Stands up straight, smiles with both eyes,
shakes your hand with a tight grip,
the same grip he shakes his dick
as he tells you to, *'just* touch it,'
as if the word *'just'*
makes it 'just'-ified
for him to satisfy
his lust
because *he must*.

What a nice boy.
He's not like the other boys you see?
Wears a belt and everything,
yet he doesn't hesitate to whip out his belt
from its resting plate before his lips are felt.
What ambition he has,
he knows just what he wants.
I'd like to pick your brains about what it takes,
To raise a man with such values and stakes,
I'm amazed a random man can devalue what
makes a soul abandon the body underneath him
and let them treat him.
Doesn't seem like the alpha type,
But he's headstrong, could be a Mr Right?

Dear his mum,
What a funny household you made
where a cold 'no' meant 'yes' to invade.
Did you blame yourself for his mistakes?
Did you cry and say you were fine?

Did he witness failed despair on your face
before you inhaled and smiled,
just for his saving grace?
When he pushes his sister down to the floor
until she's blistered and sore,
Bless him
Did you say he's a *restless one* and
his sister's provoking and poking fun.
Or perhaps you said you'd had enough,
you'd go
Right before you stayed longer with a man
whose self-importance was too rough.

Dear his father,
You fetishise masculinity in more subtle
ways than you know,
You taught him to look at women
the same way
he looks at his game;
something to win,
as if my thighs
and my words
were the goalie
for the trophy.

Please get back to me when you can
I'd love to know how you did it,
so I can raise my son with that *catch*,
so your daughter and he will be
so well-matched.

Kind Regards,

Don't mistake a number with validation,
you sell a product
and the product is you.

life is a donut
it's all circular
and everything's
just a phase
sometimes i'm really in it
and other times it's a glaze

- I'm a dick -

Truth be told it keeps me up at night
It's trapped in all the knots in my spine
I try to forgive myself rather than rewrite
all the shitty things that I cannot refine

- The Work -

I wrote down all the things I haven't liked in others.
Every bone I've picked, every joke I've stabbed at,
all the triggers I've pulled and wicked thoughts I've had.

I wrote them all down,
like each one of my fingers
was pressing into a pin board.

The list lays there,
in front of me

and there, looking up at me
were all the things
I can't stand about myself.

I'm still convinced my emotions are the weather.
(It's windy as hell and I'm feeling deep)

- Fetish for expression -

Human beings are pretty ugly
hairless, two-legged,
big-headed, a weird kinda naked.

The ones that should be adored
are human's in their truest form.
They're somewhat one of a kind.
characterful and emotional,
a rare one to find.

It's the sexiness of a soul comfy in it's skin,
When passionate, the eyes start to shimmer,
those shiny marbles tell a tale of past lives,
Wrinkles to show where they laughed and cried.
When a face moves waves of lifts and lines
one that turns a face into thousands of sides,
as they surrender to the expression that arises
No filter of how they are the feeling will confuse
the effortless radiation they bring into a room
you see it like fluidity, it's in the way they move.
It is power and humility.
this is expression.

The problem isn't *them*,
or what they said,
it's what they trigger in *you**.

Look at that.

*in most cases

You tell me I look vacant

You once validated my pain
Gave me an apology with
Promise of change

But now we sit here amongst the
Flavours of your same behaviour

So, instead of disappointment on my face
vacancy has taken it's place

- my choice -

    I want to make it clear,
    that loving you was all my idea -
    you say i'm intense,
    it's just I don't want to be
        just friends.
    It's no fuss, I got this sussed,
    I just keep my love for you pure lust.
    There's no issue, no mess, no noise;
    If I miss you and give you my best,
    well, that's my choice.

when you look out for everyone
who's looking out for you?

(I suggest you find someone who does,
or you learn how to do it for yourself)

Leave yourself as an open vessel
allow emotions to pass through.

Every feeling is at your fingertips.
You can be loving, forgiving, and true.

You have all of those resources already.

- Enter Thought -

There are layers to our growth.
It takes energy to remain awake enough
to climb through the layers into the
"innie" and "the outie"
of our universes,
in a world where
so. many. people.
remain asleep,
where we lose people
along the way, who get
trapped in a certain layer
   of   economy   or   ego.

- Enough company for one? -

I am life experiencing itself and who I am,
I should be enough company for one
but I'm not totally sure I'm content experiencing 'the me'
so alone.
So instead,
I work hard at releasing the 'me'
or experiencing the 'me' through output
so I can meet and experience myself along the way.

but then,
            I think about holding someone
all over again…

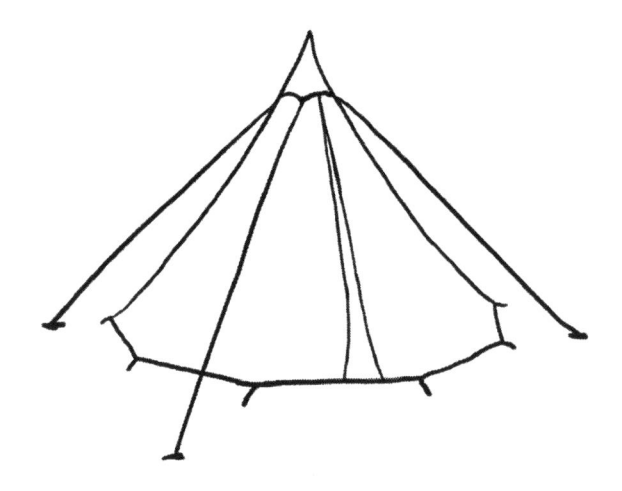

You're not defined by the feelings you have
they just temporarily 'set up camp'
within you.

My lack of profanity is a sweet analogy
of this twisted reality, a risky allergy
to all this brutality in an unknown galaxy
or it's pointless, here to annoy us.

- Your Memory -

You're more like a character formation
defects and fragments of information
locked away in my memory subconscious,
feelings I had about you,
things I saw,
but for me,
I can't say you're a real person anymore.

Can anyone else see
how much this person is struggling?
I can't fix them right now,
it's hurting me too much.
But none of their friends really *get* them, as I do.
Should I stay?

Yes, it is my concern,
because I love them.

(Breaking up with someone who can't help themselves is difficult.)

- Wrinkles -

The creases of
a life of laughter and cries
every expression felt,
of lessons and past lives.
Soft skin like thin velvet,
a silent sense of time in place.
Wisdom illustrated on a face,
in every line, a story told,
the choices made by its soul.
Don't numb your expression
because fertility is trending,
no need to conform when
you are the most profound beauty
of the human form.

if you don't "*need*" feminism
or you "wouldn't call yourself a feminist"

it's because feminism got you to a position
where you could take a position on the matter.

It means equality **for everyone.**

Until feminism applies to
all the humans in the world,
it still applies to you too.

I am you

(with a different story)

"It just is."

warm wishes

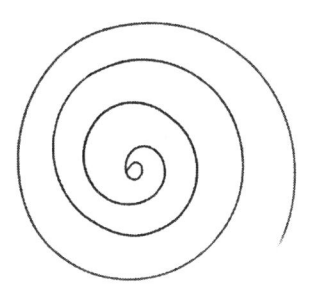

This spurt is written to you.

As I'm sure you'll gather, this was written leading up to and during the lockdown. I had an awakening to the lottery of life. How our choices and personality are reactions to our experience, knowledge, lifestyle, protection, strengths, genetics, and the particular time of life we are existing in. With this idea, every human felt immediately and existentially equal. I began to see patterns in nature that reoccurred in so many different ways. As well as seeing opposites as balance and everything in between being part of a spectrum. Spectrums could be anything from the colour spectrum, the gender spectrum, the changing seasons, light/dark, life/death, good/evil, heaven/hell, etc, everything within that has to co-exist because the opposites exist in the first place. In that way, we don't need to perceive one thing as 'bad' or one thing as 'good', it is just merely existing and thank goodness for it. There is reflection and hope in this next part.

This spurt is like cool crisp air, the little veins on leaves, and what it feels like to share a meal.

Everything is temporary.

(Including you)

- Wisdom from this experience -

    life is a series of episodes
    strung together through the senses
    society is a game
    architecture is the programming
    opposites are the same
    conflict is balance
    kindness is currency
    money is a collector's item
    enlightenment is also
    sex is perceptive
    nature is a map
    older things are examples
    people want connection and immortality
    but look for it in the wrong places
    your body is a vessel
    breathing is the rhythm of the spirit
    humans are monkey avatars
    the human race are tool-makers
    with loss of direction
    and too much power
    and time is expanding
    but full of deadlines

WARM WISHES

I am my mother's mother's mother
and my great grandchild's ancestor.
I feel everything on such an existential level
I feel for the earth and the invisible community
When a global crisis happens, it feels personal
I don't know why I'm this intense
(I just can't stop thinking about it)

In order for there to be day,
there needs to be night
The sun and moon are balanced.
Life is half light and half dark.
There has to be good and evil.

To solve the evil,
we need to address the dark side of ourselves.

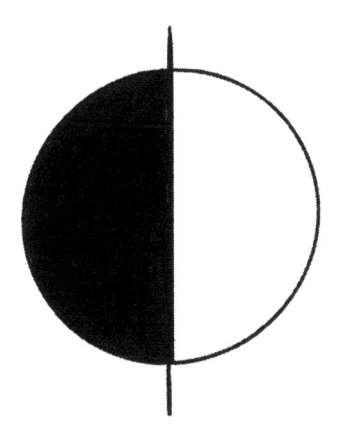

adults aren't all they cracked up to be

Thinking we're god and we're not, it doesn't involve us.
We've become excellent liars and superb at fabricating.
We are so good at talking, they say it's what evolved us
But the true evolution comes from creation
which comes from listening.

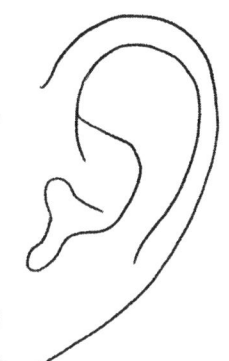

- Things that Fly -

The earth's floor, it shakes
reality forces itself awake
wrapping our mouths with masks,
to keep us from speaking.
So let us stay quiet, to listen and awake
whilst reality around us begins to shake.

They say we ate the mouth of a bat
bacteria escaped, it's released,
the frequency of earth just increased.
I could count my hand of people deceased
Your mouth is covered and your glued to your phones
Whistling sounds of birds we now call drones.
Birds of prey that live off nothing but fear
we felt we were prisoners, we had no idea
bring me to 2020 when we imprisoned ourselves,
lookout for your mouths by clearing the shelves.
Live off tomorrow, tomatoes and chickpeas
but save us some honey to medicate the bees.

- Colour In -

It's not my job to protect you
as I'm learning to protect myself

but we promise that we will
defend, honour, respect, feed and protect
the *us and our* dynamic.

that means,
I trust you won't let us down
as you can trust me

to be in a relationship
we put away ourselves and
we colour-in
our dynamic,
the us

- 'Old' Me -

what did you mean when
you told me that you miss the 'old' me?
When the real me is always unfolding,
why can't you just hold me?
I can't help that time flew and I grew.
'Old' me was just frills and tatters.

I love the 'whole' you,
surely that's what matters?

Search...

Bring me the cookie jar,
all the gooey data so far;
what I've liked and clicked,
which podcasts I picked.
The new narratives to guide
what digital realm did provide.
Give me bitcoin and fresh landscape,
virtual reality porn for escape.
I style my hair with headsets and a mic,
Reality goggles for a reality life-like.
I can *really* be me, a warrior or an elf,
Look at me, I'm an avatar of the self.
Midnight cake delivered to my door,
met the tinder match I've waited for.
Plug me up to the signal in the sky,
Give me oxygen to breathe in wifi.
See my brain uploaded to the cloud,
a cluster of captions and comments aloud.
I am my searches, my googled neurosis,
my sexual fantasies, and self diagnosis.

Watch us build in self-isolation,
The whole human spectrum
will be the new adaptation.

- DIY -

they are careless words
behind good intent
can mend anything
but themself

- A Human Complete -

I don't want a child out of vanity
or to become a mother because it's "about time"
Or for the sake of spawning another
to the already growing population
of ignorant and shallow followers

but...

If I had a daughter
It would be to start again.

My wisdom and wounds
and the most beautiful seeds of myself
would cluster in my womb.

I would rest my belly on a bed of silk,
feed from nut milk and berries.
Watching seasons change in motion
while I coat my foetus in warmth
and devotion.

My veins as roots
watering my
blossoming earthling.

Her pulse
would be the first beat
of the anthem,
The ground would shake
and she'll emerge,
A mind untouched
by ego, greed, and expectation.

Let her
palms press into the points
of my fingers
to push herself up,
And her body
weigh upon my feet.

I would untie the tight restraint
around her ankles
that held back the women before her,
Kiss her head
and put the world at her toes.

Allow no projection to taint her
or the regrets of her mother
to change her.

She would be born with
fingernails to cut water
and legs to leap obstacles.

Her appearance merely the shape of her vessel
than something that would be compared.

She'll know her body is a temple by ten
and that only she has the clout to use it.

When she opens her mouth,
I would assure that people listen,

I'll teach her how to love others
as herself
but never to love another lesser
than herself.

She would posses all her own resources
mentally
soulfully
and physically,

I would feed with her self love
until her heart's too thick to break.

My child
My fresh start
My perfect pieces reincarnated;
un-compromised
untainted
unpolluted.
My full potential
personified,

                A human complete.

- Let's make self respect sexy again -

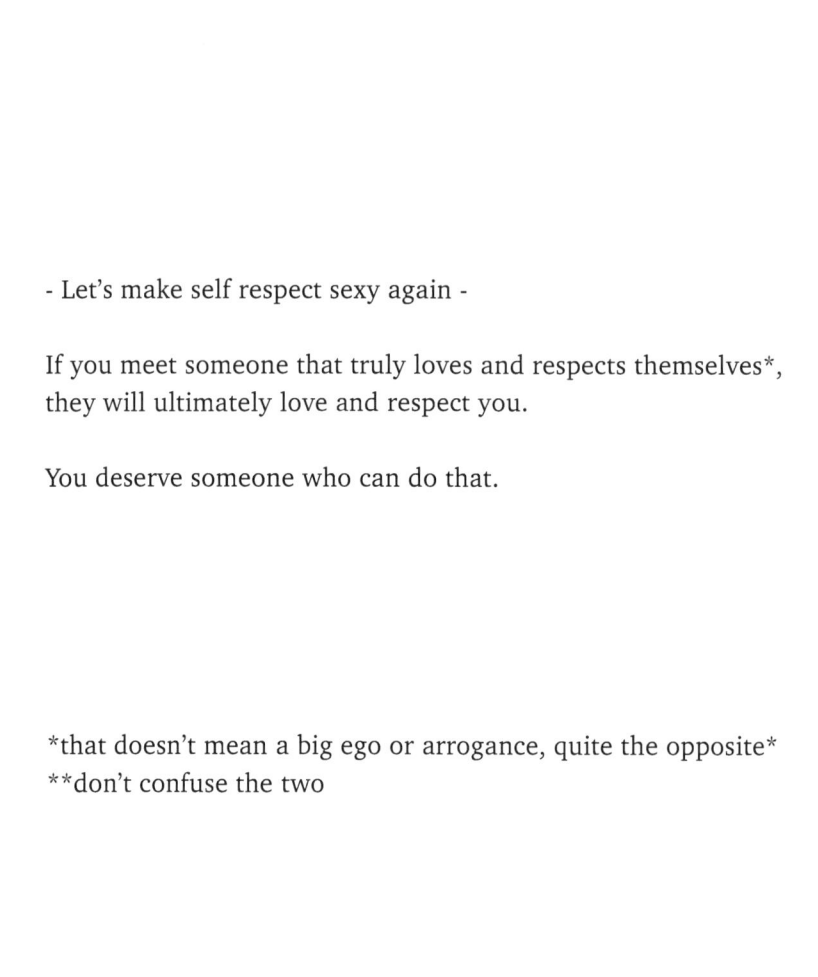

If you meet someone that truly loves and respects themselves*, they will ultimately love and respect you.

You deserve someone who can do that.

that doesn't mean a big ego or arrogance, quite the opposite
**don't confuse the two

- How Life Happened to You -

They said to themselves, craving for connection,
"it's sparse and empty, let's add to the collection.
Something is missing, perhaps it's time we should,"
so he licked her belly and fantasised of fatherhood.

Every day she hoped it would be soon
she prayed for one bloodless moon.
Her belly became bulbous and purpose grew,
he turned to her and said, "that'll ground you."

(I never understood, Is it having sex or the wait,
that people can't help but congratulate?)

Then out came a being, something to project,
finally something to carry, smother and protect.

Sorry for the unprepared life you've occurred in,
Never once did they consider the burden.

What if,
that's not the thing
I'm grieving over
but rather

the idea of life itself?

Because now,
without that,

I remember
life goes on

- How it was before -

Haven't we been practicing for years?
to make individualism our careers?

Worshiped money, jobs, and shops
then suddenly it all comes to a stop;
all the structures we knew,
Is all threatened by a flu.
We wanted more and more
now we want it "how it was before."
Well welcome to our biggest fears,
a mask tightened around our ears
Our smiles are now hidden behind.
The new and changing mankind:
We have to forget and reset.
Don't look to 'before', but how 'it will be'
whatever world we want to see.

So fill yourself with purpose and love
the only thing we'll need more of.

When I was an infant
I kept wondering
how the night stars were hanging.
What put them up there?
Tied tight with a knot,
All other realities dangling,
so still
like eyes.

"Look up,
look up"
she says,

'up' in our atlas
she said,
'like dreamcatchers'.

- Utopia -

Welcome to our very own utopia!
stepped off from the brink of dystopia
So, we lost people along the way
now the empty streets call for a new day
we stopped all plastic and went zero-waste,
stopped methane pollution with plant-based
No more 'buy now and bin later', we recycle
We went all electric, encouraged to bicycle
We dress in second-hand clothing for fashion
'love thy neighbour' became our compassion
turns out that the ego has no place.
goodbye to the world as a rat race
we evolved with each other and grew
adverts will now be hand-written and true
understood peace over war is more appealing
So we planted seeds for food and healing
All weapons, war, and trolling became undone,
Imagine feeling close and kind to everyone.
We play to our strengths without competition.

This is utopia, so let's make this the mission!

- Reporters -

We are the same thing
all here
at the same time.

The only thing that divides us is
experience.

We should think of each other as reporters.

Reporters sharing
our
observations
of
life itself.

- A Bundle -

you are the curling ladder of DNA
you carry from your ancestors

      your spine holds notches
      of all trauma and culture
      you've inherited

            you are a bundle of unique
            and valuable experiences
            fed to you by your senses

                  you are all the choices
                  and decisions you make

                        You're inherently
                        unique

You're worth my dead arm

- to my other spoon-the cost of true mindfulness is forgetfulness

we are all a collective mind
a hub of consciousness

it starts with the individual
in the same way that one bee
contributes to one big picture

different hives
different life spans
Devoted to pollen
all the bees produce one output

like any movement,
it starts with you
and me
today

the way we respond will affect the taste
of our honey

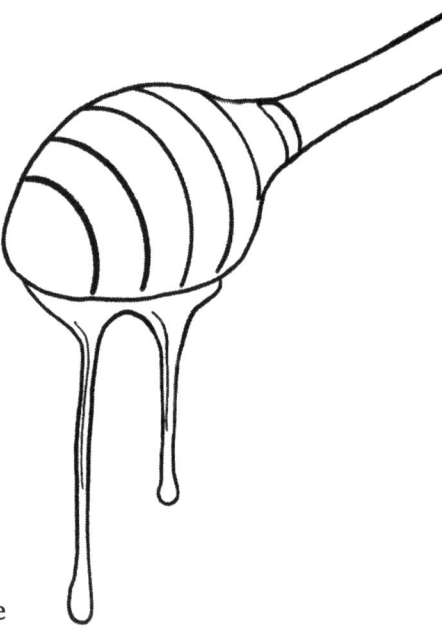

(Is this a good poem? I don't know.)

algorithms are designed to glue us
glue us to our phones,
So they sell us more
to want what *they* have
so we spend more
so we fund more useless products
and pockets of useless people
We create the social disparity
we claim to detest

capitalism uses our egos to make money,
and addiction is the key

- Maleness -

Maleness is trailing through layers like it's raving
It's harsh and it's cold and treats power as its sold
it's soul harnessed by it's own hold,
seeks its fate because it has ego to uphold.
But masculinity in it's pure form forms shapes like it creates
Feels like divinity sidetracked by storms and
misunderstood and left detached.
With norms of tribal brotherhood
and fatherhood like strong-armed cuddles
born into deep reliance for any struggles
a bond between men is a tight alliance
A tent pole of the house hold,
something to fight for a steadiness
as defiance, it's mental headiness
but the opposite is a war, a fucking crisis
makes the group amongst it frightened
it's not what has been fed to us
Masculinity meets femininity
like two halves are the whole
the meeting is an infinity
we blend all our roles
They say the rising of the sun
is the thrivin' of the masculine
the glowin' protector, growing
and synergising, pollinates it's nectar
and its energising,
warms it's creations,
endorphins of elations and
full of intentions
Vibrating inventions,
it's temperamental but passion
building all that energy experimental
Masculine needs re-defining,
looking at its linings of logic,
its drumbeat deeply erotic
Machismo is a mind like an arrow

too sharp, precise,
decisive but narrow.
Direction of the dart
replaced love of the heart
because an eye on the prey
are eyes left astray
they say it's the hunter mentality
but that's a fallacy, an excuse for raw brutality
a sexual appetite that's pure carnality
When the real masculine sexuality
is kinks of mountains and dances
around wet fountains,
it fills spaces and links,
Nor their desire craved by life
has been weakness used as a weapon
the maleness is more accepting
not the effected and reactive
slaves as we were made to believe
nor so fussy for the female form
to be so perfectly perceived.
There to relieve all the fantasies we feel.
Dionysian persuasion grabbed maleness
Fizzled it into an equation entrapped
all it's pain and made leadership an authority
where lack of tears became shackles of fear.
Built structures of science and competition,
became a priority
made false smiles and impulse an ambition
Tangibility are restraints on the profound power we can allow
Let us untangle the chains that hold this masculinity down
Allow it's beauty to be shown
Unshackle ourselves from what we know
Maleness is profound,
it is also misunderstood.
It is an intrinsic part of ourselves,
when male spectrum
is half of life itself.

- the entanglement -

like roots strangling one another
earphone wires tangle in each other
sweatiness and wetness
squelching as we restrain ourselves
and threaten ourselves
and all reframe from mini hells
too much self-reflection to ever really 'flirt'
as we wear trauma like it's a stained shirt
day's pass us by, that's history concealing
Everywhere it sounds like little people screaming or
perhaps it's those people over there, still singing?
Twisting our back like it's a sack of
cracking bones when our body's wringing,
preventing our fleshy parts from tingling
Got to wring out our ears,
and all our past coding
Ear wax, gas, and skin
don't last, they're eroding
the beats in our breathing lungs
feeling clung to all our impulses,
knowing around us is all just falseness

Why you should self-reflect on what you say and do:
To learn more about yourself,
to correct your mistakes,
to become a better person
to connect you better with others,
so you'll be happier.

What you do to others, is what you do to yourself.
Our external reality reflects our inner reality.

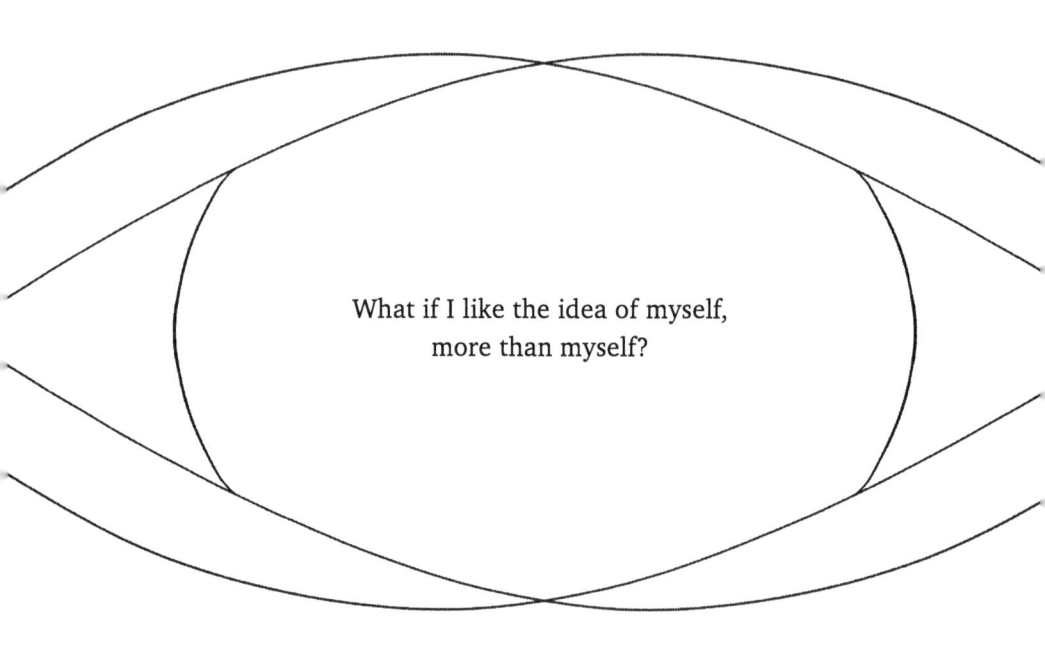

What if I like the idea of myself,
more than myself?

- EGO -

In your stories, you're always the hero
Letting yourself go to the ego
Doesn't rating yourself give you a clue?
Aren't your anxieties tiring to you?
thinking your word is your law
Secretly thinking you're free of flaws
Repeating them stories is a bit of a bore
With each restraint your souls getting sore
Look at you, obsessing over the material
When you could be blessed with the ethereal

●

the ego reacts,
lies,
and protects itself.

Who is the "you"?
Do you define yourself with your
gender, politics, past, your inked skin,
The colour of your hair, the money you earn,
The role you play, the ambition you live by?
Do you limit yourself to a constructed idea?

your ego is made up by you

the 'you' is entirely dependent on
the choices you make

You made up the ego,
so let it free

you share matter, time and energy
with everything else on this earth.
Your experience is your uniqueness

You definitely exist and that's ~~enough~~ incredible

When you think of all the planets
time zones, centuries, past lives,
countries, dimensions,
layers of consciousness, places, spaces,
all species and dreams.

Right now,
we're here together.

You're looking at me and I'm looking at you.

We're life looking at itself.

- The end of the world poem -

It's just like any other day
except the people are all praying
Clouds are all swirly
going to them heaven gates,
hope they're pearly
It's the end of the world
see, life's ripped and it's
truly hurting
time and I were just flirting
It's all a curse
we don't even get a hearse
and all
all this youth was no rehearsal
    but it *all* seemed so personal
wet eyes drying because they stared at it.
reality around 'em starts tearing
it's all those thirty-somethings screaming
but this is the feeling
fear of death here
a kind of relief
fuck any belief for now
folks are getting rowdy
folks remain strangers
it sort of pains you
stops you refraining
    because all we were doing
    was playing
    trying to create a self
    wanting some help
    and craving to be held
    making up this realm
TV says it'll all be a flame
three hours left to claim

hey to the people I never met
I pray your extinction is a harmless death
data blocked due to over access
before it just crashes,
> I tried calling you and I didn't get through
> it was just to assure you,
> I wonder who warned you.
> If you were with me,
> I'd pull a mattress out,
> to the nearest grass
> I just found
> I'd feel the ground
> watch the sky melt
> wish it was your hands I felt

eyes closed like it's a birthday wish
Silence is the new life sound
other than biblical verses from
some dude in a gown,
all prestigious
a man shouting the sermon,
life for the religious
was just an excursion
a practice round for those reincarnated
wish I'd found something like that,
I kinda craved it.
Heaven awaits through this blurred vision
> but my last thought is that I miss him

like when you miss a train
but it's just hit me
> I definitely spent most of my life
> binging on that lonesome gratification
> and now its time for the ultimate annihilation
> I guess I took the latter
>> *did anyone actually know me?*
>> *Maybe it didn't matter*

my turn to go turned up pretty early
life so quick,
only took a toke
of all that secondhand smoke
so swirly, filling up my lungs
and petty silver linings
wrapping 'round my throat
So many people
had me mistaken,
Barriers are down
and there's no faking
This is the smell of extinction
Now we'll burn like bacon
Nothing we haven't done
Before it was all forsaken
    I wish I had loved everything more
    It just always felt like a bit of a chore
    and way too difficult
    'suppose it felt like a trick and all
    curse of thought and a conscious mind
    Got me feeling like I was the unusual kind

remember:

It's more important to hold hands than wash them.

- vote -

Vote for us!
UK and US,
a vote for
property and poverty
we possess
Do you want the
wealth and borders,
the oil and limbs
we hoarder?
Welcome to a dog-eat-dog place
a world we love to call a rat race.
"do what you do best, look after your self
don't stand too close and clear the pasta shelf."
This is one salesmen's tip that we do
make the decision to buy feel made by you.
An algorithm has followed you for years,
realised soon you're posting all your fears,
if it makes us angry or sad we care,
One bad thing and 'click', we share!

We became hateful and sad in our darkest hour,
we disagreed on Brexit, trump and pussy power,
We spoke of free speech and not to consume,
then kept our distance and quarantined in our rooms.
When we butcher the animals that walk the land,
we become the bacteria we *so* want banned.

(a meditation for you)

>Switch it <u>all</u> off,
>
><u>just listen</u> to your breathing.
>
>*What is it telling you?*
>
>*What's your rhythm like today?*

- Listen to all the sounds outside of you
- The closer sounds
- The sound of your body

>Look at you meditating.
>
>Be aware of being aware.

- This is stillness.

>ature<u>Observe</u>, breath.
>
>Every exhale is *a* <u>release</u> from the body
>
>every inhale, you welcome in a newness.
>
>What feels better?
>
>Breathing in or breathing out?
>
>All thoughts, memories, regrets & desires
>
>are merely illusionary in *this very* moment.
>
>All you really know, and all you will ever know
>
>is that the moment happening <u>right now</u>
>
>is the only real thing you have.

{Look around you now,   realise it,   breathe it in}

This is a reality, an experience, somewhat a miracle.

And you are here too.

This is life happening
with you in it.

they had no idea,
that these are the
best days of
their life

spending it
mending
what feels like
the ending.

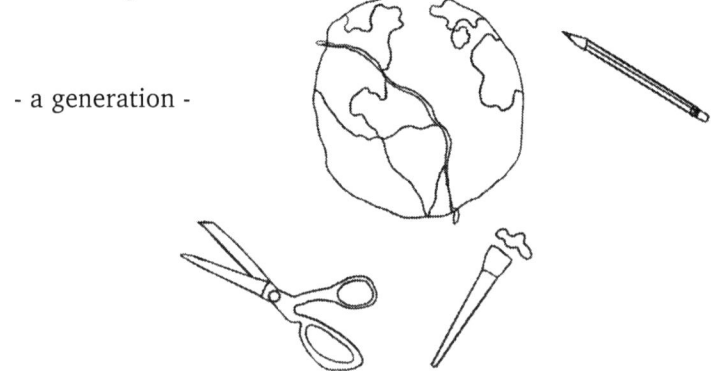

- a generation -

- It's gone viral -

The world has been corrupt by a deadly virus that threatens to scar us -
Our insides, our lives and rots the lungs that we breathe from
Bacteria sits on our tongues that made us question our freedom
I know we're all contagious, potential carriers
So we cage away and put up our barriers
Because I'm feeling it I swear,
and I must have caught it from somewhere

The commercial getting me itchy desires, telling myself, 'let's try this'
'Maybe I'll just buy this'
It's a twitchy compliance,
It's all enticing but I don't want to get misguided.

But what's the point of saving our lives when we ain't even living right?
They're right. Our immune system is fucked when our minds don't even fight
The infection began in my throat when my silence become a compliance
Trickles down to the pit of my gut, puts me mind in a rut, it must be the virus.
Now I'm feeling homesick, for a home that doesn't exist,
home is the place where I resist,
but I've got symptoms and it's on the list.

This disease of lack of instigation, is spreading over a global nation,
TV with no real conversation,
a need for instant gratification,
Don't talk to me about germination when the lack of solution is a violation.
When strangers walk away to make a space for social distance got me feeling rejected.
Masked up, space made and homeless more neglected,
They ranked us in priority got us feeling so selected,
it's the mind that's infected,
watching the TV thinking, *who the fuck have we elected?*

Who really cares? It ain't those billionaires,
buying their products, making their money,
unethical practices destroying the country.
Consumption is contagious, when buying doesn't phase us,
commerce and company: When *all we want* is company,
looking for community or some friends
Thumbing our screens for the latest trends,
When we have an acronym for FOMO
It's because we see other's lives as a promo.
There's a bug in our bodies when our lives are used for data,
Seeing perfect lives wrapped in perfect lies, *rate him, rate her*
Plagiarising our needs, our mannerisms
Splattering our mucus onto algorithms
A world where posts with fake ass get more attention
than our attention can span.
I don't need to be good at reading humans to see the cracks in anthropology
Convinced we're made of skin of weak bodies and a mind full of ideology
See, there's an outbreak of categories,
we read the books but we don't see the allegories,
Poisoned by our insecurities,
thinking we claim territories.
When the venom makes me believe my worth is my credit score,
I'd be saving my life so I can live life like their impartial corpse.

It's the same disease that's got us logging our track and trace,
Whilst the people who matter care more about a race to space
We're conditioned in a culture that's protected by vultures burning our pockets.
while they're firing up in phallus-shaped rockets fuelled by profit.
You can avoid all the brutality when you're off to the galaxy.

It's hurts me to see how fast you can act when you think your life's in jeopardy,
but when our planets turning and forests burning there seems to be no remedy.
See this is my future, my life, my air, *so you see*, that just offended me.

Parent's now watch a 'How-to' for a response to their babies screams,
before they wrap up their faces and glue their eyes to their screens.
Toddlers with iPads, teens and their fads, adults skipping ads, *it's just sad*.
There is an outbreak and it's entertainment that is going too far,
It wasn't a coincidence that the president was a reality star.

It's no mistake that this illness makes you tired,
Makes you lose a sense of being inspired.
It's people who create that loose,
they don't stay safe,
they're just suddenly erased.
I ask the authority to tell me how art isn't a priority
Life in monochrome without colour is just duller,
Subdued in its meaning, interpretation and rudder.

So what am I offered?
I'm offered alcohol, cigarettes, chocolate, suppressants,
the doc is filling out prescription for anti-depressants,
feeble medication and now they want my arm for a vaccination.
You can't tell me you really care about what's attacking my cells,
When you ain't offering anything that the pharmacy doesn't sell.
Deprived of nutrition information, no healthy living education
No therapy suggested, no vitamins or mental health,
We just sat around and watched Jeff Bezos get more wealth.
Tell me, how the hell am I supposed to agree,
When news claims there's no benefits from vitamin D?
The sickness that believes that PHD's - and - wise honesty are somehow linked -
It's believing in those PHD's and science geeks that made us lose our instinct.

You're protecting the community and that, but there's no community in isolation
"Protect yourself and clean the shelves" - - I say,
deliver us from temptation and send us some help.
Vaccinate me from a lack of transparency, hypocrisy and inefficiency
Because when it comes to clarity, we're now in a deficiency.

It is from them that this illness has dispersed,
A curse that the fish rots from the head first.
So be sure that we got this virus from them,
They're decisions in our systems like phlegm;
The apathy, the thirst, mistrust, and violence -
Divided, silenced, a total lack of guidance,
Our choice to separate from the environment.
We're sick and it lives in language used in their speeches that appear,
The words of poetry that they choose, the leaching vocabulary of fear.
It's of anger; the disbelief of their ability to feel love's intensity,
No belief in the consciousness trinity, …a distrust in the infinity.
They send out notices of the virus, spooning us a dose,
When it is them that needed rescuing the most - -
'I'm sorry no one saw you, nothing stepped in to cure you -
before the <u>tight hold of ego</u> became your affliction
And you chose fight to power to be your addiction.
Now you push it on us through money, competition, fame, and lust.
Ah! The flu must've blocked you from seeing that <u>you're the same as us</u>.'

I stop to remind myself, "No, this is all to save our lives,"
but how can I believe that when male suicide is on the rise?
When sugar and alcohol stands in front of me, advertised?
And the stats say how many black lives have innocently died,
When domestic violence increases and is still set aside,
When the concept of sustainability is used by a franchise,
And speaking of spirituality is still somewhat stigmatised.
I open up my third eye and ask again, *is this to save our lives?*

Can I get better? When awareness brings frustration,
That frustration holds inside of me, another ego-formulation
Maybe I should leave it, find peace of mind and hope it fades
Perhaps the revolution of wellness comes from giving aid
through my conversation, my celebration, my meditation,
through my listening, assisting and persisting.

Move my attitude to pure gratitude
Recovering with purpose, presence and peace,
Use my illness as a mouthpiece
Not to please, but instead, to release:

That the world has been corrupt by a deadly virus that threatens to scar us -
Our insides, our lives and rots the lungs that we breathe from
Bacteria sits on our tongues that made us question our freedom
I know we're all contagious, potential carriers
So we cage away and put up our barriers
Because I'm feeling it I swear,
 and I must have caught it from somewhere.

I don't believe in a God
but I do believe in life itself.

I believe in us,
I believe we understand pain
I believe in the present moment
I believe we meet important people
I believe the universe shows us things
I believe the pleasures of life are a gift
I believe nature is smarter than all of us
I believe this reality is an interesting one
I believe my mother's instinct is to love me
I believe I am an extension of a bigger thing
I believe in the changing seasons and plant life
I believe in loving someone more than yourself
I believe that eyes are more telling than we know
I believe in the mathematical patterns being a clue
I believe in all the opposites of life creating a balance
I believe in all the insects and animals that fertilise this earth

(add to the list)

it was nothing before you were born
it's nothing when you die
life's just the excursion
between birth and death
Raise a glass to those I never met

imagine if you were born,
never been in this world before,
no idea of the ability of sight,
sound, touch, smell and taste
everything you saw was new
interaction was all play
we used to say,
'Imagine if'
and
'let's pretend'
We had passions,
and so many
to befriend.

Mirror children and all young things
The world is still new to us
We can be more playful and affectionate
Less self-conscious and more expression felt

It's as if one day I'll wake up from this reality and think, "of course that was a dream, it was ridiculous"

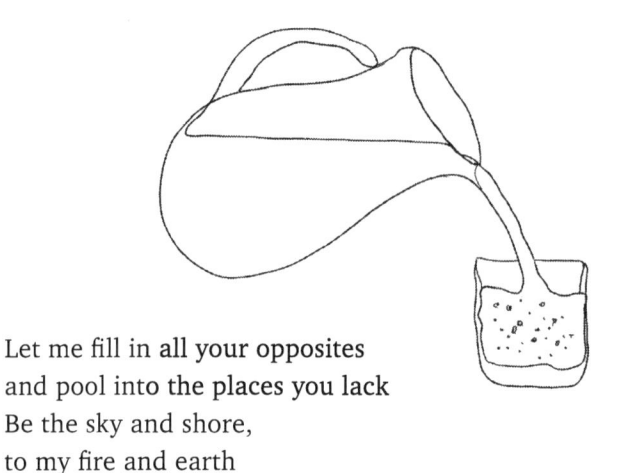

Let me fill in **all your opposites**
and pool into **the places you lack**
Be the sky and shore,
to my fire and earth
as if we were two halves
torn.

Let's pretend we are two halves of society
the human spectrum divided into two.
Let's prove to ourselves and each other
that we could be a whole,
at one with itself.

- every interaction you have -

when you understand that you are
the everything and the nothingness,
you are free.

Freedom gives you choices.

You choose:

- your state of being
- your reaction
- your words
- your opinion
- your identity
- you

every time you reflect, remorse or regret
or stop your mouth from spilling a come-back

You peel back a layer into enlightenment

life happening in front of you is a miracle,
$\qquad\qquad\qquad$ it's *all* just miracles

*(to all advertising companies who need a slogan, I am available for hire)

It's never a copy and paste
as so much about me changes,
as I go through phases
change shapes and faces
it's all seasons and paces
But it is my essence
that stays in place.

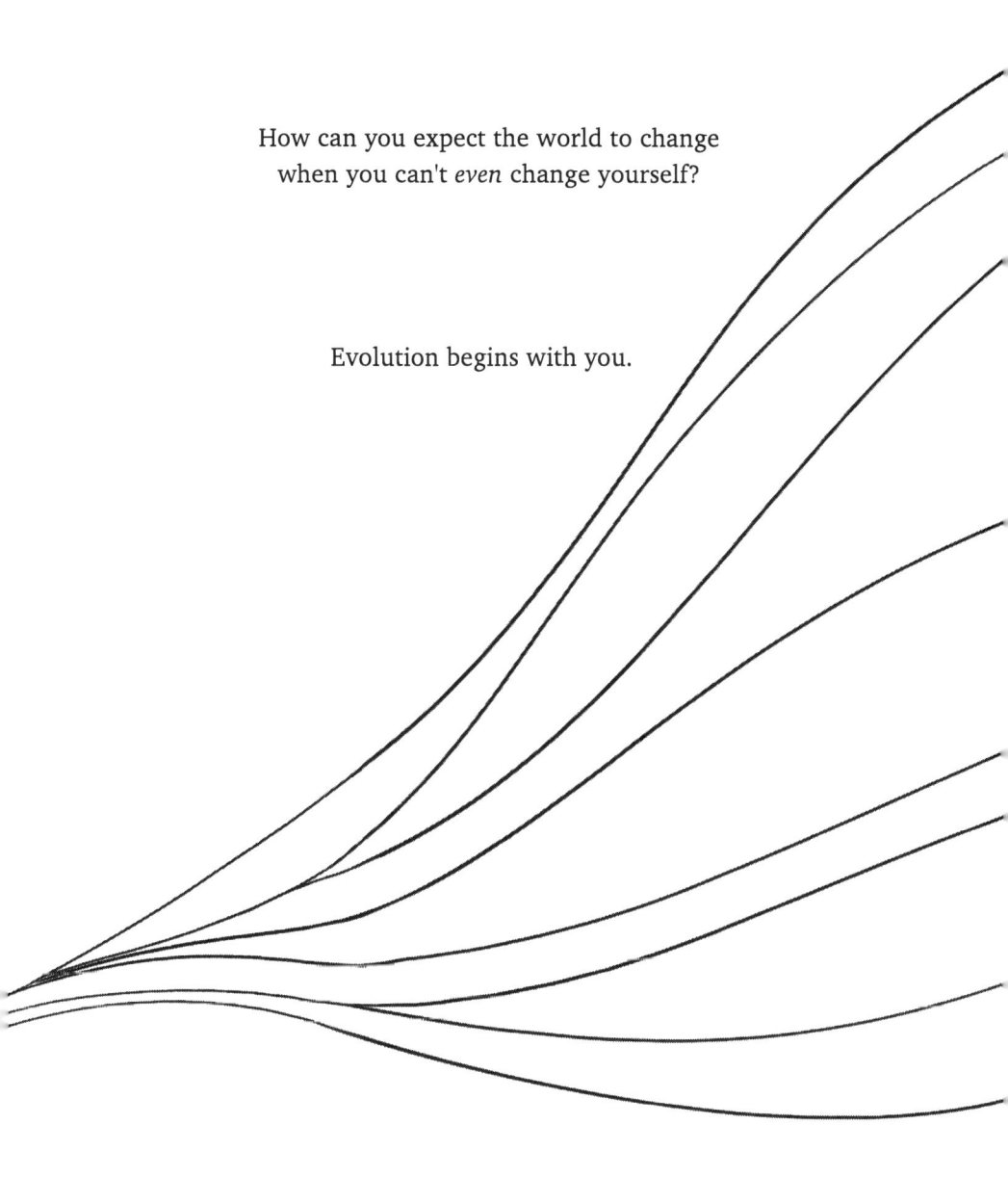

How can you expect the world to change
when you can't *even* change yourself?

Evolution begins with you.

notes from your mind

I am so deeply grateful for you reading this book, thank you! It would mean the world to me if you could leave your honest review online!

Connect with me on Instagram
@elizapitkin

Printed in Great Britain
by Amazon